SELF-CONFIDENCE WORKBOOK FOR WOMEN

*Start Owning Your Self And Reignite
The Exceptional Woman
That You Are*

Marcee A Martin

© Copyright 2023 - All rights reserved.

The content contained within this book may not be reproduced, duplicated or transmitted without direct written permission from the author or the publisher.

Under no circumstances will any blame or legal responsibility be held against the publisher, or author, for any damages, reparation, or monetary loss due to the information contained within this book, either directly or indirectly.

Legal Notice:

This book is copyright protected. It is only for personal use. You cannot amend, distribute, sell, use, quote or paraphrase any part, or the content within this book, without the consent of the author or publisher.

Disclaimer Notice:

Please note the information contained within this document is for educational and entertainment purposes only. All effort has been executed to present accurate, up to date, reliable, complete information. No warranties of any kind are declared or implied. Readers acknowledge that the author is not engaged in the rendering of legal, financial, medical or professional advice. The content within this book has been derived from various sources. Please consult a licensed professional before attempting any techniques outlined in this book.

By reading this document, the reader agrees that under no circumstances is the author responsible for any losses, direct or indirect, that are incurred as a result of the use of the information contained within this document, including, but not limited to, errors, omissions, or inaccuracies.

ii | *Self-Confidence Workbook for Women*

$129 FREE

Achieve a Worry-Free Smile with these
12 Mental Health Books!

The Easy Way to Improve Mental Health

Therapy doesn't have to be so expensive and complicated. That's why we are giving you these 7 eBooks and 5 bonus workbooks so you can start improving your mental health right away, without leaving your home!

- **Stop Worrying All the Time**: Stop those nagging thoughts in their tracks with mindfulness and anti-anxiety tips expert CBT therapists use!
- **Do Therapy Your Way**: Start taking action with 5 BONUS workbooks, so you can start smiling, laughing, and enjoying life on your own!
- **Love Yourself, Love Others**: Enhance your career, relationships, hobbies, and more as you march through each day with confident self-esteem

Scan to download:

Table Of Contents

Introduction 1

    Dear Reader 1

    Mirror Mirror on the Wall 2

    The Key to Confidence Lies in Feeling Truly Worthy................ 3

    Let's Go Deeper to Bring Out Your Self-Confidence................ 4

    Succeeding With Confidence Is an Ongoing Commitment........... 4

    Planting the Seeds of Self-Confidence................................ 5

    The Self-Love Workbook 6

    Summary of Chapters.. 7

**Chapter 1: Understanding the Core of Self-Confidence
for Midlife Women** 9

    I Just Packed Up and Moved to Ireland 9

        The Magic Combination of Confidence and Self-Belief........... 10

        What Are the Reasons That May Be Holding You Back?........... 12

    What Does Self-Confidence Look Like at Midlife? 13

    Feeling Lousy Doesn't Have To Be a Permanent Thing in Midlife 14

        Create Your Own Positivity Magic Spell Every Day 14

    Creating New Behavioral Patterns...................................... 16

        Say "No" Out Loud 17

    The Importance of Breaking Negative Habits 17

        Hebb's Law and the Power of Creating Change Through Healing...... 18

        The Power of Healing Your Thoughts and Behavior............... 19

        How To Use This Book.. 20

    More Tips for Using This Book 21

    Seeking Help 21

Marcee A Martin | v

Exploring the Definition of Confidence..24

    Confidence Defined For You 26

    What is Prime Confidence? 27

Key Takeaways...30

Chapter 2: Why a Person Might Lack in Developing Self-Confidence.......31

Owning Your SH*T!..32

    Learn From Experience About What May Have Knocked Your Confidence33

The Benefits of Self-Confidence...35

Factors That Negatively Impact Confidence 39

    Feeling Like You Have To Be Perfect..39

    Disapproving Authority Figures...41

    Childhood Issues and Trauma 41

    A Negative Work Environment..44

    Your Personal Beliefs 46

    How Can You Tell if You Have Healthy Self-Esteem?....................50

    How Does Low Self-Esteem Manifest in Your Life? 51

    Excessive Self-Esteem Is Not Healthy..51

    Here's How You Can Improve Your Self-Esteem 52

Key Takeaways...54

Chapter 3: Setting up the Right Mindset for the Best Foot Forward........55

The Natural Success Mindset 55

    Feeling Deserving of Success..60

    Tips for Building a Positively Successful Mindset 60

    Controlling Intrusive Thoughts 66

Keep This In Mind About Midlife 72

Becoming Unstoppable..77

Worksheet for Improving Your Mindset...79

    Mental Exercises To Train Your Mind To Become Unstoppable! 79

    Mindfulness Practice 81

    Yoga and Meditation 82

    Getting Into Shape 83

    Creating Healthy Daily Habits 83

vi | *Self-Confidence Workbook for Women*

Chapter 4: Removing the Dark Side: How To Remove the Bad Programming Inside Your Mind **85**

Understanding Your Potential..85

The Midlife Reflection...90

The Golden Rule..93

The Destructive Emotional Baggage...95

    Reducing Negative Emotions...95

    People Pleasing Cancer..97

    The Unhealthy Side of Codependency 99

    The Magic of Making Mistakes..102

    Reducing the Overthink...105

    Eliminating the Fear From Within...109

Key Takeaways...113

Chapter 5: How the Top 1% Thinks **115**

Work is Love Made Visible 115

The Great Secret to Success and Being a One-Percenter...............116

The Genius and Luck Combination Work Like a Charm...................117

Follow Your Heart and Act Without Hesitation...............................118

Follow Your Inspiration 120

Your Desire to Succeed Must Be Stronger Than All External Factors 121

Use the Power of Authenticity to Change Your Life 122

The Push of a Little Confidence Will Reshape Your Destiny............124

Don't Wait for the Perfect Conditions for Success To Arrive 127

Living Life With Purpose..129

The Natural Abundance Mindset 131

The Power of Shifting Perspective...133

Key Takeaways...136

Chapter 6: Getting the Fuel..**137**

The Driving Force 137

Getting Unstuck From Your Comfort Zone.....................................138

Finding Your Purpose 141

Marcee A Martin | **vii**

Worksheet for Developing Your Driving Force 143

Key Takeaways 145

Chapter 7: Working on the Foundation of Self-Confidence 147

Control What You Think About Yourself 147

Our Thoughts Are Vibrations That Become Our Reality 148

Determining the Values 152

The Link Between Conflicting Values and True Happiness 153

Organizing Your Values 156

When Values Don't Match Anymore 156

Key Takeaways 158

Chapter 8: Worksheet To Improve Your Purpose and Personal Power 161

That Revisited Integrity 161

Achieving Peace of Mind 164

Explore Your Spirituality 166

The Initial Stages of Creating and Manifesting Our Experiences 168

Let's Aim To Improve Our Vibrational Frequency 169

The Universal Laws That Regulate Life in the Best Way 169

The Law of Attraction 169

The Law of Concentration 170

The Law of Correspondence 170

The Law of Substitution 171

The Law of Emotion 172

Power of Decision 172

Key Takeaways 177

Chapter 9: Competence and Personal Mastery 179

What Is the Limit 179

Inspiration Like Lightning Strikes Unannounced 180

Designing Your Ideal Work-Life 181

Articulate Your Vision in Broad Strokes 182

Identify Your New Interests and Areas of Excellence 183

Identify the Goals You Want to Achieve Over the Next 5–10 Years 184

viii | *Self-Confidence Workbook for Women*

Tips to Stay on the Path of Your Goals 186

Key Takeaways 187

Chapter 10: Working With the Deep Game of Self-Confidence 189

The Law of Belief 189

Being Your Own Cheerleader Increases Your Self-Belief 193

Developing Strength and Resilience 194

Tips to Improve Your Resilience 195

Key Takeaways 197

Conclusion 199

About the Author 201

References 207

Marcee A Martin | **ix**

INTRODUCTION

Everything you experience emotionally begins with a thought. –Marcee A Martin

Dear Reader

As I walked into a room full of enthusiastic midlife women ready to start the next best chapter in their lives, I hardly recognized the woman in my shoes. She was smart, brilliantly confident in her stride, and brimming with enthusiasm at the prospect of making a difference in the life of many other midlife women facing similar challenges that she herself once faced. In the past, I cringed at the thought of speaking in public. My palms would get sweaty, and my heart raced so fast, I could barely get the words out of my mouth. I had little confidence in my ideas and spent endless hours riddled with anxiety as I cared more about what other people thought about me and my ideas than I did about myself. Today, I own my ideas and feel differently about so many things. I hardly recognize this strong, beautiful midlife woman in my shoes, who walks with a bounce in her step. She takes amazing care of herself, isn't afraid to go after what she wants, and just loves the feeling of waking up to a brand new day to shine her light in the world.

Oh, but it wasn't always this way for me. There were some mornings as I approached midlife when I just couldn't get myself out of bed.

I felt sick in my stomach thinking of all the time I wasted clinging to negative thoughts and beliefs about myself. Yes, life has been a mixed bag of emotional highs and lows for most of us, and for me too. I know firsthand how hard the lows can hit your confidence levels. It can strike us down to deep shameful feelings of inadequacy. I've experienced that over many years. I wished many times that it could all just go away. I am sure you can relate to this on some level. It was easier for me to think negative thoughts than positive ones when it came to myself.

For many years I had no idea how to change that. I just wanted to feel like the sun was shining for me when it mattered the most. On most days it felt like it was shining for everyone else but me. However, I did not give up on myself. Somewhere beneath the surface of all that negativity, was the young girl who still believed in magic. She is that same woman who walked into a room full of women to inspire them and show them how they can own their SH*T to reignite the badass women they truly are. Today she is grabbing each brand new day with both hands, walking and speaking with confidence, and she is in control of her thoughts, feelings, and life, completely!

I realized that we have the magic within us to change anything that we want to about our lives. Even though I could've chosen to remain in the black hole of self-doubt, self-hate, and self-pity, I decided not to. It was my true self that finally fully emerged from within to lead me on this newly inspired path. It was the light of my soul that guided me back to my natural confidence. However, I needed to work on myself to improve my level of contribution. I realized that it was my mind that was sick. It needed healing, love, and care. If you can relate to my deep past feelings of inadequacy, fear, and anxiety, then you too can take the necessary steps to heal your mind, body, and soul. There's no better time to get started than at midlife when your second Spring is upon you as a woman.

Mirror Mirror on the Wall

When you reach midlife, looking in the mirror, what do you see? Do you see yourself as being smart, capable, beautiful, and wise? Or do you still see yourself as a woman of regrets and heartache? Do you feel worthy of your achievements, or are you still playing small, while holding a half-empty cup in one hand?

You might have been put down by people close to you, those whom you trust and love. These suffocating feelings of inadequacy have affected your psychological and emotional health for many long years as it has mine. It is time to turn your life around, to make the best of the second Spring of your womanhood. Now at midlife when looking in the mirror what do you see? A woman of power, confidence, and wisdom or a woman who always gave herself less of a chance at anything she wanted to pursue?

On the other hand, are you fairly content with life, and do you feel that you've done enough, achieved enough, and most importantly that you truly valued yourself throughout your journey despite the unique challenges that you faced? I am sure that your answer is not a full YES to the last question. If this is true, then sit back and get ready to change that as we journey together to the core areas of your life still riddled with negativity.

The Key to Confidence Lies in Feeling Truly Worthy

The worst part is that you may not have been consciously aware of everything that impacted your confidence levels in the past. Just like me, you may have just sadly accepted passing challenging moments as truth, and internalized those negative experiences. When we do this, negative experiences do leave a more lasting impact than we care to admit. I suffered from these moments of deep anxiety myself, for many years. My greatest realization came in midlife. After investing much time in improving my overall self-image I now know what I wish I always knew.

We do have the power within us, to put an end to negative cycles of anxiety, stress, and deep sadness. I will show you how to achieve all of that in this book! You will also learn that success is not a settled matter. It depends on how you think and feel about yourself. Surprisingly, unlike what most people think, success has little to do with external achievements and everything to do with your internal perceptions, thoughts, and feelings. The bottom line is: Success is changeable at any given point in time, based on how good you are feeling about yourself from within!

Let's Go Deeper to Bring Out Your Self-Confidence

This entire book is an invitation to go much deeper into your subconscious mind, to unlock all the negative traps you've set for yourself over the years. After working through the inspiring and revealing exercises here you will start moving on from "I am not good enough," to embrace a more abundant mindset that leaves you feeling deserving of happiness and success. I label that mindset as "Confidence!" When you are mindful and consciously aware of how everything serves you for your highest good and growth, you will increase your level of confidence. When you heal from the past and use those experiences as a springboard for further growth, you will feel more confident, and self-assured about your personal identity. The journey we are now embarking on is about getting to this destination:

> Experiencing higher levels of confidence, success, and feelings of worthiness! When you understand that the "midlife crisis" is really an awakening that can also be regarded as a blessing, your confidence will outshine any regrets that may be holding you back in life. You will also experience more love, gratitude, and success.

Succeeding With Confidence Is an Ongoing Commitment

The commitment we are now making as we begin this exciting, life-changing journey together is to awaken the idea in our consciousness that unless we believe that we are worthy of success, it will remain elusive. You will achieve it once you start unlocking the traps in your subconscious mind that have kept you stuck in a place of doom and

4 | *Self-Confidence Workbook for Women*

gloom about your prospects. Unless you feel naturally more accepting of yourself regardless of your challenges, you will need to rethink the quality of your life, and the quality of your thoughts. You see, how you measure success really depends on how meaningful your life feels to you at any given moment in time.

It is not important how the world measures your success. It is important how YOU measure your success. Confident people already know that they are always worthy of success, regardless of their circumstances. This is the reason confident people will always set out to achieve everything meaningful to them in their life. They will do whatever it takes to be happy, and fulfilled, regardless of their age, and regardless of the amount of money they have in their bank accounts. That person can be you!

Planting the Seeds of Self-Confidence

The journey behind you has also left you with a yearning to get more out of the remaining years of your life. Of that, I have no doubt, as a midlife woman myself who has just transitioned successfully to get more from the remaining years of my life. It is this midlife yearning we will uncover together to bring it to full manifestation. Together, we will plant the seeds of self-love and self-confidence, as you work through the mind-shifting exercises set out lovingly here. Your mind is like an internal feedback mechanism. It does let you know when there are unresolved issues that need your healing attention. We will explore the feedback that you are receiving now in your midlife transition and use that as a signal to create the much-needed change that you crave.

Over the years, your level of awareness has broadened and this is the most blessed and exciting part of reaching midlife. You have more to offer now than you ever did in the past. If you had half a chance in your twenties you can own it completely in midlife! This book has purposefully come into your life with this important message:

> You deserve to own everything that makes you unique and
> you must permit yourself to feel passionate again from the

depths of your soul. If you stick with the journey for the next 30 days and fully participate in all of the transformative exercises set out here, your determination will soar to new heights. The power is in your hands.

As a woman, you are powerful, in your own right. Everyone is powerful by nature, to be an expert in their destiny at any age. It is the mindset and hurtful experiences that have created some disillusionment for us. We feel the sting of that disillusionment when we reach midlife. All the false expectations, fantasies, and regrets can fall by the wayside now as you reclaim your personal power, and get ready to experience the best years of your life.

The Self-Love Workbook

As you have already learned in my first book of this Midlife Women Series: *The Self-Love Workbook For Midlife Women: A 30-Day Healing Journal: Release Toxicity, Overcome Self-Doubt,* I too had to do the work on myself to reach full confidence in my abilities when I reached midlife. I was determined to start fresh, to own my past issues, and to heal them. This allowed me to make space for newness, freshness, and aliveness that is refreshingly inspiring and peaceful.

I also know that the hormonal imbalance we experience biologically at midlife impacts our behavior at times, as you previously discovered in our journey together. This is why the self-love journey you embraced in my first book was an important stepping stone to regaining your full personal power.

Stick with your healthy self-care journey, the one you created in your Self-Love Workbook, and get ready to amplify your personal transformation in this amazing, empowering second book of my series. I would love to hear from you, so do write to me at the following address: hello@ marceemartin.com. It would be wonderful to connect with you. Your feedback is valuable and much appreciated.

Summary of Chapters

Chapter 1: We begin our powerful journey together uncovering what confidence looks like in midlife, it is a somewhat different picture to what it looked like during your earlier years. However, some positivity magic can reduce the impact of lower estrogen and progesterone. Learn new ways of creating more positivity in your life.

Chapter 2: Understanding the value of confidence can help us to shine a light on those things from our past that may have knocked us down! It is time to heal those issues and to own them completely. Learn how to set yourself free from the past.

Chapter 3: Low self-confidence is a reflection of a defeatist attitude. The opposite of this is feeling deserving of success and abundance. We call this the natural success mindset. You can develop this and become unstoppable!

Chapter 4: The midlife awakening is seen as a blessing in disguise. That's because we know intrinsically that it is time to release the darkness that has been keeping us stuck in playing small. Learn how to let the light in.

Chapter 5: Your desire to succeed at something must be stronger than all the negative factors stacked against you. When that happens magic is created. Discover this power as you explore the success enjoyed by one percenters.

Chapter 6: Getting out of the comfort zone is just one of the challenges faced by midlife women. However, all it takes is a spark of inspiration to fuel you up and send you off into the domain of new possibilities. Discover your driving force in this chapter.

Chapter 7: In this chapter, we take a deeper look at the impact that negative thoughts and beliefs have on our choices and destiny. Also, get ready to reclaim your power, and own your new values in midlife.

Chapter 8: Be inspired by the Universal Laws studied over centuries. Learn more secrets to success, and discover how to harness your

Marcee A Martin | 7

energetic frequency by choosing thoughts that relate directly to all that you want to manifest in your life.

Chapter 9: Inspiration is like lighting. It can strike at any time. You must therefore have a clear plan in place and always be open to receiving inspiration on your path to greatness. You will create your blueprint for success in this chapter and obtain absolute clarity on what you want to go for in midlife.

Chapter 10: We end our journey by looking into the mirror once again, to count our blessings and plant the seeds of hope!

CHAPTER 1

UNDERSTANDING THE CORE OF SELF-CONFIDENCE FOR MIDLIFE WOMEN

Be brave to rediscover yourself at midlife, and let nothing stand in your way from embracing a new vision. –Marcee A Martin

I Just Packed Up and Moved to Ireland

Anne Driscoll was 62 years old when she decided to pack up and move to Ireland. It was the first time in her life that she decided to do something as spontaneous and big as that, with full belief in herself, not entertaining any doubt. After never living outside of Massachusetts, Driscoll instinctively followed the nudge of inspiration from within when the opportunity arose. It all started with one random casual conversation with a colleague. She was always drawn to Ireland and felt a connection, but she didn't have the confidence of looking further into it. The thought of finding work and moving there seemed impossible to her. Yet somehow it made sense and happened when she decided to look into a new possibility that emerged at a random conference that she attended.

As a journalist, Driscoll loved stories but felt defeated at the idea of finding work in Ireland. She shelved the idea until that synchronistic event presented itself to her. Driscoll was at the Investigative Reporters and Editors conference when she chatted to a journalist friend who casually mentioned that she had just returned from Ireland after completing a Fulbright scholarship there. This changed the trajectory of Anne Driscoll's life.

At 62, Driscoll still had it in her to get excited again about the prospect of moving to Ireland. Had she been stuck in the mindset of being past midlife, and worried again about the details involved in moving, Driscoll would not have taken the plunge to find out more and see what her chances were of succeeding this time around.

The Magic Combination of Confidence and Self-Belief

It was the Fulbright scholarship that gave Driscoll a new roadmap for her life. Age is only a number when you are alive and open to the idea of new possibilities. She used her inner drive, and confidence in her abilities, and became enthused about the idea of moving to Ireland once again. This time, Driscoll did not give up on herself and came up with the idea of teaching law students at the Irish Innocence Project at Griffith College in Dublin.

Using her journalism skills, Driscoll decided to teach students in Dublin ways to investigate wrongful convictions. Ambitiously, confidently and with a newfound sense of determination and commitment, she put together an impressive five-page proposal and a two-course syllabus. Driscoll was accepted and successful! The college invited her to stay on even beyond completing her Fulbright scholarship. (Sinrich, 2023)

Do you have a dream, or an idea you feel drawn to but keep shelving it out of fear or lack of insight as to what options may be available to you? What are those ideas, and why have you not pursued them?

Marcee A Martin | **11**

What Are the Reasons That May Be Holding You Back?

Write it down here, and rethink those excuses you've been making. Perhaps it's time to re-examine those ideas and come up with a new roadmap! At the very least if you still get excited by these ideas, open your heart to them again. The possibilities are endless once you tap into them with confidence.

What Does Self-Confidence Look Like at Midlife?

We must be upfront and clear about this. Self-confidence looks slightly different in midlife than it did when you were in your twenties. That's for sure! The midlife transition is a unique journey, one that every woman must adequately prepare for. Learning more about the changes that your body undergoes will empower you to do what is required to lessen the impact of those changes. All those details have been outlined concisely for you in my first book: *The Self Love Workbook For Midlife Women: A 30-Day Healing Journal: Release Toxicity, Overcome Self-Doubt.*

This is where you will find all the information you need on the biological and physical changes every woman faces in midlife. If you have any questions whatsoever or would love to share more about your self-love journey then feel free to email me here: hello@marceemartin.com. This second book now in your hands will elevate your understanding of self-confidence, and show you how you can get the most out of your midlife years.

We have already learned from the first book that hormonal changes create imbalances that can have both physical and psychological consequences. To recap the most pertinent side effect: Declining estrogen and progesterone levels are largely responsible for a whole range of midlife symptoms in women. The perimenopausal and menopausal symptoms can also impact your mental health in the following ways (Nhsinform, 2022)

- anxiety and irritability
- anger
- intense mood swings
- sadness and depression
- loss of self-esteem
- loss of self-confidence
- poor sleeping patterns
- poor concentration

Marcee A Martin | **13**

As your body undergoes these dramatic biological, physical, and hormonal changes, you are bound to experience some psychologically associated challenges. Your confidence will also take a knock in the process. All transitions we go through in life involve painful psychological realizations. However, once you earnestly work through these challenges you will get back on your feet to experiencing full confidence again. The point is to own your "discomfort." When we do this we become accountable and it is then that we can accept the imperfect nature of being human. It is empowering to own your struggles completely and unashamedly.

Feeling Lousy Doesn't Have To Be a Permanent Thing in Midlife

It is important to keep in mind that just because you may be feeling lousy now and then, it does not mean that you're not good enough. It is part of the midlife transition and it is also part of being human. We are emotional beings as much as magical beings with extraordinary abilities to achieve the impossible. Accepting these moments as "passing encounters" reduces your chances of permanently internalizing the negative thoughts associated with midlife mood swings.

Create Your Own Positivity Magic Spell Every Day

Remembering to flip the switch of internal dialogue from negative to positive during these midlife mood spells will definitely make a difference over a period of time. Why not create a new inspiring midlife spell of positivity? You can achieve this by surrounding yourself with inspiration daily and by creating a magical self-care routine that works for you. It will push out the negativity.

That's what spells are all about, manifesting more of what is important to you, and less of what is not important to you. Beautiful things, scents, and more natural elements are just the ingredients we are looking for. Confidence is about feeling good all day long, if you can help it. So let's add a dash of magic every day to improve how we feel about ourselves.

Add more beauty to your environment or home, bring out the fresh-smelling lemons, and lavender around your home and office, listen to inspiring and calming music more often, have a massage, or just go out for a scenic walk in nature when you recognize the onset of a midlife negative mood taking over. The power is always in your hands.

Flipping the switch from negative to positive every time you are facing a negative thought or challenge, will gain momentum and soon you will be listening to more positive internal chatter. It will change the trajectory of your life, giving you all the confidence you need to stay on the path of self-love.

Never underestimate the power of breaking negative habits to replace them with new inspiring ones. The first step you take towards eliminating negative thoughts which associate your self-image with "I am not good enough and I am also beyond my prime years," is a powerful first step forward into a brighter future.

The Basic Ingredients of Your Daily Magical Positivity Spell

- Surround yourself with inspiration every day.

- Listen to inspirational podcasts or watch one inspirational video. Read an inspiring book every week.

- Listen to calming music. It can be classical, Zen, relaxing instrumental, or the sounds of nature. Do this while you work or during your rest in between. Take regular breaks from your work.

- Practice daily meditation in the morning and preferably in the evenings. Use a timer to take small five-minute meditation breaks in the day or even one-minute meditation breaks to release negativity.

- Surround your environment with beauty and the healing fresh scents of lavender, lemons, and rose. Whatever fragrances work best for you will do. These scents are very uplifting.

- Take time out to look at nature. Go for a walk or a quick jog, or a refreshing swim.

- Watch the sunrise in the morning and enjoy a relaxing moment out in nature as the sun sets after a productively inspiring day in your life.
- Use your imagination to create and improvise on your daily magical positivity spell.

Creating New Behavioral Patterns

Breaking bad habits to replace them with better choices is important. What it does, is it replaces the old habit, completely eliminating the negative consequences associated with the behavior. We already know how our health can improve when we decide to quit smoking, for example. In this case, better choices that replace old negative thinking habits will also have a positive impact on your life. Forming a new behavioral pattern in your brain to replace the old pattern is what we are aiming for.

The more steps you take towards improving your level of self-confidence in midlife, the better your chances are of improving every area of your life, just like your health will improve if you stop smoking altogether (if that was one of your bad habits). It is not always easy creating new habits because our minds and body have been conditioned in a certain way to accept the old ones. However, you can achieve great results when you stick to the new healthier choices that you are making for yourself.

Anything you set your mind on achieving can be done. It's a question of believing in your positivity spell. Keep applying it as a magical new encounter. Just don't give up on yourself when things get hard. You will have those weak moments, and there will be times when you might relapse into the old pattern of thinking and reacting. When that happens be kind to yourself, and remind yourself that tomorrow is another brand new day to get back to your new healthier patterns of thinking more positively about your life.

If you ask anyone who has given up smoking how they feel now about their health, and how it is impacting all areas of their life, their answer is not hard to guess. It usually includes, "I will never look back and regret kicking that habit. It has changed my life for the better now!" Confidence and success can become a settled matter if you are willing to start letting go of all issues from your past that may still be bringing you down. The decision to get started is a powerful first step.

Say "No" Out Loud

I too had to start from somewhere to get my life in order during my midlife transition. Deciding that I had enough of living my life being stuck in the depths of emotional whirlpools due to all the negativity I bombarded myself with over the years, was the first powerful step in a new direction for me. So deciding to start new habits is not a small matter. It is a gigantic new step in the right direction. It will help you to break free from internal negative patterns hardwired in your brain.

Say "NO" out loud when that negative internal feedback mechanism kicks into effect during those midlife low mood swings. Transforming your life from the inside out requires you to be fully present in your mind and your body, to listen and feel everything that is going on inside of you. Bring out the magic by dispelling those negative thoughts and emotions.

Send them out to the Universe for healing and begin writing a new chapter of your life. Decide to be more of your magical self and choose more enchanting, and powerful new thoughts about yourself. The same logic of saying "NO" applies to anyone and everyone who is struggling with a bad habit. Negative thinking is a bad habit! You need to take active steps forward to rewire your thinking and behavior habits. (Pychyl, 2012)

The Importance of Breaking Negative Habits

It was Canadian psychologist Donald Hebb who famously concluded in his study of the human brain: Neurons that fire together wire together. This also explains the fundamental law of neuroscience. That being, the brain is more susceptible to changing thought patterns that were once believed to be true. This is great news as neuroscience has further enlightened us about the power of human consciousness and our ability to change anything we want in our lives when they no longer work for us.

We can change our minds about anything, including how we think about midlife and how we feel about ourselves. You can think your way to success if you are serious about feeling more successful and being more successful in any area of your life. Hebb's Law lies at the heart of understanding the link between the brain and human behavior. (Beins, 2022)

Hebb's Law and the Power of Creating Change Through Healing

Hebb's theory stresses the importance of repeated behavior to create new neural pathways in the brain. The process of learning and unlearning involves repeated action and behavior. This is how neurons are activated to create a "paradigm shift in thinking, feeling, and human behavior." When you repeatedly flip that switch from negative thoughts or self-defeating ideas to being more positive, and resilient to challenges, as well as being more supportive of your midlife journey, you will achieve breakthroughs!

Repeated behavior results in the strengthening of connections between neurons which wires your brain in a new way. Once positive habits are hard-wired in your brain, being more positive and learning new skills will become second nature to you, just as it did when you were learning to ride a bike or drive a car. The bottom line is that you can rewire your brain through repetitive behavior, and take repeated action in the direction you wish your life to follow. Emotional circuits are also formed in our brains when we repeatedly respond in the same manner to situations.

Our brains are firing and wiring neurons which strengthens old and new patterns of thinking and behavior. When you no longer reinforce old habits, the circuits weaken and fade over time. When you take active steps to heal from the past and start looking back on those events as an observer or witness, the emotional charge will also weaken. This is how

18 | *Self-Confidence Workbook for Women*

you practice mindfulness. You become an observer, to heal, understand and form new resolutions based on new insights and breakthroughs.

The Power of Healing Your Thoughts and Behavior

It is through this practice of developing mindfulness, that we can change our thinking patterns. When we do this, we also become more accountable for our present and future happiness. You will naturally learn to forgive yourself and others in the process of this healing. Sometimes the ones we love the most may have hurt us unconsciously. It is important to keep this in mind. Just like you, they too are on their own journeys. Always bear that in mind, it increases empathy and helps us to maintain a level of objectivity in our dealings with others.

However, your priority is to shift your thinking patterns from blaming yourself for everything bad or challenging that has occurred in your life. The purpose is to release those past negative emotional connections from your mind and YES your body, which stores them. While it is natural to question how we could've done things differently, always remember that you did do your best under the circumstances based on your limited experiences and knowledge in the past.

This book is designed to help you in this specific manner. The self-reflective work that you are doing here and in the entire series dedicated to midlife women, are designed to help you to heal, achieve clarity about your life, and take full control of your remaining journey. You are tapping into your memories, to reclaim parts of yourself that you may have ignored or forgotten about.

Having come this far in life, you deserve to acknowledge your entire journey as a meaningful experience. Every part of you, even the discarded parts of you, makes up the whole picture and has contributed to your thinking and emotional patterns. Working through your past issues will empower you in a new and enlightening way. Also, when you begin to nurture yourself more and practice self-compassion, your neural pathways are changing to reflect this new behavior and response to yourself.

Marcee A Martin | **19**

Once you start achieving breakthroughs in your journey you won't feel so bothered about a lot of things anymore. You can be more authentic and really go for your dreams with a full tank of confidence. Your awareness of yourself will improve tremendously, as you strengthen your ability to transcend the things that are no longer relevant. You will also be more confident in your ability to make better choices in every moment and to assert yourself when necessary.

How To Use This Book

Your full participation will help you to achieve clarity and go deeper within yourself to achieve breakthroughs, insights, resolutions, realizations, and new goals. Answer all of the questions and don't hold back from being honest with yourself and your feelings. There is no one watching you or judging you. This is your journey and every bit of honesty will help you to heal, and to become your own best friend.

If you find that you have become stuck in one place while developing or trying to develop your self-confidence, reflect on the reasons why you may be feeling stuck, and honestly examine those reasons. Make a note of those reasons. You may not feel this way throughout your journey, but only when dealing with certain issues. Highlight those issues that may be holding you back from progressing with building your self-confidence. Don't resist it, but acknowledge it as being a true reflection of where you need to do more work, to find more answers.

Let those answers come from within until you find resolutions that feel right for you. We are all unique and have different paths and ways of healing. Take a break if necessary to fully resolve an issue through meditation or writing, or listen to calming music to release any stress. Trust your instinct and move on as soon as any anxiety starts to subside and ease its way out of you. Take a walk in nature or go for a refreshing swim to also let go of pent-up energy. It feels good to exercise. It will help to clear your mind. As soon as you feel better, reconnect with this journey.

More Tips for Using This Book

1. **Following the guidelines that are mentioned in this book.** Everything in this book is designed to help you see things as being on the way and not in the way. Do the work, and explore the journey of your midlife transition. Fully participate and be enthused about the learning outcomes.

2. **Setting the right mindset.** Be energetic in a way that supports your learning. Cut out distractions and see this learning opportunity as being your time with yourself to improve your outlook about midlife and to take your journey to the next level of achieving healthy confidence in yourself.

3. **Taking it with proper consistency.** Be consistent and complete the entire book in workable bite sizes to achieve maximum results. You can decide what will work for you and how you will commit to completing the entire book. You can set aside 30 minutes a day or 60 minutes a day to give good thought to the content in each chapter. Work through each practical exercise in a way that is not rushed but thorough and authentic.

4. **What to expect.** A learning encounter that is informative, inspiring, and sensitive about your journey and the changes you are going through now at midlife. You can expect to transform your life, and mindset, and continue the healing journey we began in the first book: *The Self Love Workbook For Midlife Women: A 30-Day Healing Journal: Release Toxicity, Overcome Self-Doubt.*

5. **Important considerations.** Your daily schedule must be taken into account. Things may come up for you that could take you away from your time here. Deal with priorities but stick to completing this book and not jumping to something else once you sit down to do the work here.

Seeking Help

1. **Where to seek professional help.** If you feel strongly that you need professional therapy to help you cope further with midlife,

then go for it. Find a professional mental health therapist who specializes in helping midlife women in your area, or close by. You can also connect with someone who has been recommended online if this helps. Ask questions about the process involved, and trust your instinct when making a decision.

2. **In whom you can confide.** You know your friends and close family members best so trust your instinct about people. Only confide in someone with whom you're comfortable. It does help to have a friend around you to confide in. Maintaining a high-quality social life where there is real sharing and caring is a wonderful way of staying inspired.

3. **Which resource is authentic and which is not?** Trust reliable sources of information on the internet that are provided online by qualified mental health professionals, when looking for medical advice. It will also be great to connect online with other midlife women on their journey of midlife self-discovery. Read widely on the subject or any other relatable niches for the information you need to further help you in your journey of regaining full confidence in yourself.

What would you love to achieve from this book? It is important to write down what your goals are with regard to building confidence in all areas of your life. Look at your current mindset, observe it, and reflect upon it. Begin with the end in mind when setting out to accomplish any goals in your life.

Explore your answers below here:

---

22 | *Self-Confidence Workbook for Women*

Marcee A Martin | 23

Exploring the Definition of Confidence

Now that you've learned a bit more about the mind in the previous section as well as the role that positivity can play in your life, it is time to improve your understanding of "Confidence!" Can you think of moments in your life when you felt on top of the world, so completely that it felt like there was nothing that could stand in your way during those moments?

List all those wonderful moments in your life where your confidence led to magical outcomes. Fill the list below to the last line. Think of every moment when you experienced confidence in yourself.

1.	*For example:* When I decided to speak up and share my ideas with the team, because I fully believed in them, and bought into those ideas authentically myself.
2.	
3.	
4.	
5.	
6.	
7.	
8.	
9.	
10.	
11.	
12.	
13.	
14.	
15.	

16.	
17.	
18.	
19.	
20.	
21.	
22.	
23.	
24.	
25.	
26.	
27.	
28.	
29.	
30.	
31.	
32.	
33.	
34.	
35.	
36.	
37.	
38.	
39.	
40.	

Confidence Defined For You

Confidence largely determines the level of success you will experience in your life. It is a direct reflection of your belief, and faith in yourself. This also corresponds to the amazing results you can create for yourself in your life. If you are feeling confident, and happy, you will experience moments of bliss. Athletes usually describe those moments as being "out of their bodies," or feeling an inspiring lightness. When you are confident, it strengthens your ability to make strong, powerful, and meaningful decisions for yourself. It also anchors you in the present moment.

You feel alive, on fire, and with purpose. The amount of confidence that you will experience throughout your life does ebb and flow and largely depends on so many different factors. However, keep in mind that you do have the final say over how you think and feel, and therefore you are powerful to determine the outcome of any challenging situation. Once YOU decide that you are ready to win your game of life, the level of confidence you feel about your potential will ultimately be the driving force behind your victory. When you get to Chapter 5 of this book, you will learn more about how self-confidence and belief work like magic to shift your destiny.

If you're very talented and skilled but fail to believe in those abilities, your chances of achieving success will dwindle. There would be a greater probability that you will fall short of achieving your greatest potential. Earlier in this chapter, you met Anne Driscoll who always dreamed of moving to Ireland and you discovered how having confidence in her abilities eventually resulted in her realizing her fullest potential and dream at the age of 62. Also, she was excited about the prospect of examining a new way of manifesting her dream. That energy with confidence helped her to land a job in Ireland and it opened up a great opportunity to finally move to Ireland.

When you're confident, inspired, and you trust your instinct all at the same time, amazing things can happen to you. Similar magical things have happened to many people who suddenly received flashes of

26 | *Self-Confidence Workbook for Women*

inspiration and felt an excited confidence emerge from within. They had the courage finally to explore those flashes of inspiration and to witness its manifestation into amazing results in their life. Confidence comes in short bursts of excitement from within and it also sometimes requires more effort. If you achieve consistency in your level of confidence you will have more flashes of inspiration and you will undoubtedly transform your entire life to reflect your true desires in midlife.

What is Prime Confidence?

This is where the magic occurs when confidence becomes a spiritual encounter. You can think of this kind of confidence as the remarkable ability to overcome any setback because you believe in yourself regardless of external labels such as failure, loss, or heartbreak. Your resilience in challenging situations will therefore manifest the true level of confidence that you feel about yourself and your abilities. Ultimately we should all aim to achieve this level of confidence in ourselves. It is a very deep and lasting faith to have in yourself.

A person who is deeply confident in themselves is also someone who has a great deal of compassion for themselves and others. Even if it is the small voice whispering to you that tomorrow you can try again when you're down and out with no one to turn to for help. That kind of spirit will get you through tough things, and your mind will naturally embrace new possibilities and you will not give up on finding better ways to achieve your goals. The power of the mind is what will set you free from your suffering. As long as you believe in yourself, you will find ways to persist and overcome anything! That is what having prime confidence in yourself is all about!

When you accept a setback confidently as a challenge to overcome without trashing your self-esteem in the process, that is a result of possessing prime confidence. A person with prime confidence believes in themselves whether they're winning or not. Any victory that you experience is also measured by factors internally that either have value to you or not. Similarly, any failures you experience are also processed as something of value or not. When you start thinking like this, you will always be a winner, knowing that winning or losing is only a matter of perception.

When it comes to the midlife transition, having prime confidence means that even though you might be going through some very low emotional moments, deep down you know and you still believe in yourself, and you will not surrender yourself completely, but take things naturally in your stride to persist to live your best life possible (Taylor, 2009). If I could change anything about my past, it would be to not have been so hard on myself during setbacks. We must aim to exercise more self-compassion and keep moving forward without knocking ourselves down psychologically when things don't appear to be working in our favor.

Do you have what it takes to be a person who exudes "Prime Confidence" in herself? When in your life did prime confidence get you through a major crisis or when in your past do you wish you displayed more prime confidence, that could've saved you a lot of emotional energy spent in the wrong direction?

_____

_____

_____

_____

_____

_____

_____

_____

_____

_____

_____

Key Takeaways

- The midlife transition is a unique journey, one that every woman must adequately prepare for.
- Learning more about the changes that your body undergoes in midlife will empower you to take the right action.
- As your body undergoes these dramatic biological, physical, and hormonal changes, your confidence might take a bit of a knock—it doesn't have to be a lasting encounter.
- We are emotional beings as much as magical beings with extraordinary abilities to achieve the impossible.
- Remember to flip the switch of internal dialogue from negative to positive during those negative midlife mood swings.
- Surround yourself with inspiration daily and create a magical self-care routine that works best for you.
- Decide to be more of your magical self and choose more enchanting, and powerful new thoughts about yourself.
- You need to take active steps forward to rewire your thinking and behavior habits.
- The brain is more susceptible to changing thought patterns that were once believed to be true.
- Once positive habits are hard-wired in your brain, being more positive and learning new skills will become second nature to you.

In the next chapter, we will look at the benefits of self-confidence and some of the reasons why people experience low self-confidence.

CHAPTER 2

WHY A PERSON MIGHT LACK IN DEVELOPING SELF-CONFIDENCE

The power of love can heal anything that we touched with fear in the past. –Marcee A Martin

Now that you understand how midlife can impact your level of confidence, let's examine other factors in your life that may be responsible for your experience of low levels of self-confidence. These factors could be related to past challenges, setbacks, and experiences. Unless we were born with an internal confidence that can withstand everything when it happens to us, most of us have experienced low levels of confidence under very challenging circumstances in our lives.

Having low self-confidence could be linked to other things that are not related to menopause at all. However, reaching midlife could be a "trigger of old emotional responses" to unresolved issues from your past. When you feel low due to menopausal symptoms, it can be worsened by overthinking issues from the past which made you feel lousy as a person.

Some of these issues may have been buried deep in your subconscious mind to avoid dealing with them altogether. It may have been life experiences that you wished away and suppressed dealing with at all. Sometimes we want to block out past experiences altogether, because of the psychological pain associated with those experiences. However they do resurface at a subconscious level, and these unresolved issues do impact our level of confidence. Those unresolved issues are bound to come up during the midlife transition and will inevitably make your journey even more profound as you are forced to relive those experiences in your subconscious mind before finally laying those old ghosts to rest. Our past can haunt us for many years unless we change that!

Owning Your SH*T!

Whether you care to admit it or not, anything that you bury deep in your subconscious mind, or ignore out of feelings of shame, anger, or regret does impact your level of confidence and hence your self-belief. What you may be afraid of and slightly ashamed of must be confronted. Escaping is only a temporary reprieve. There is nothing to fear about what is no more in your life. The past is over. It is only the residual emotional experience that remains. Energy can be shifted within us when we are willing to do the work to shift it and convert it to positivity. It is time to shine your healing light on the past, to release negative emotions still stored in your memory and in your body.

This is how we heal and finally transcend from those experiences all the more wise, compassionate, and powerful. Owning your SH*T means proudly acknowledging that some things that happened to you in the past were great while others were not so great. The bottom line is that you pulled through everything and that is what counts! The past is long over and done with. We cannot change the past. We can heal it.

Always keep this at the back of your mind: Terrible things happen to the best of us, and it is nothing to be ashamed of at all. All we can do now in midlife, as mature wise women, is to nurture that inner child and let her know that she did her best always under the circumstances based on her level of awareness, knowledge, experience, and limited understanding. Remind your inner child how beautiful she always was and tell her that you are sorry that you didn't always believe in her. Let your inner child emerge in your consciousness now, and send her all the healing light and love she always deserved to receive during those not-so-good encounters. Do that to all the parts of yourself that you discarded, and send them love. All those parts make up who you are, so they are all worthy of your love, and wisdom today.

Learn From Experience About What May Have Knocked Your Confidence

Think about those experiences from your past that may have hurt you or destroyed your confidence in some of your abilities. Remember, that being vulnerable is the same thing as opening your heart to let it all go, to release it from your system so that nothing will stand in your way again. Getting things out of the way will help you to see yourself fully, as you are now, with your strengths, and your capabilities. Self-reflection helps us to view our experiences in life in a new light. It does help to clear things up once and for all. You were always worthy of love regardless of what you may have done or not done in the past.

34 | *Self-Confidence Workbook for Women*

The Benefits of Self-Confidence

- **You will be more successful and happier in life:** Let's face it without self-confidence our lives will be dull, and uninspiring, and we will not be able to reach our fullest potential. In midlife, self-confidence is the silver lining in the sky, offering hope, and renewed enthusiasm to seize new opportunities with both hands. During this important midlife journey, when you commiserate about your life, it is important to be confident enough to value yourself, your uniqueness, and your entire journey without negative labels. Remembering your life's journey as a reflection of growth, progress, and transformation is a confident way of approaching midlife.

- **Encourages high self-esteem:** How you think and feel about yourself impacts your attitude. How you think and feel about yourself also depends on your personal belief system. Being confident naturally about your personal identity regardless of the unique set of challenges you have faced will be a boost to your self-esteem. Confidence encourages us to continuously regard our self-esteem in all situations. Healthy self-esteem is supportive of your journey.

- **You can hold your head up high:** And own your SH*T regardless of the opinions of others. You have the wisdom now to understand that no one enjoys perfection. It is non-existent. Producing excellent results in all areas of your life is about confidence, having a positive attitude, and possessing the ability to continuously bounce back when the going gets tough!

- **You will be able to enjoy the little things in life:** When we are confident, we are happy with ourselves. When you feel good about who you are, you will be able to enjoy the little things that bring you joy, without nagging thoughts of negativity or self-doubt. When you experience those moments of joy, you will continuously feel an inner sense of liberation. You will smile more, and look forward to doing everything you love doing, no matter if anyone else shares these joys with you or not.

- **Decreases self-doubt completely:** Believing in yourself is a powerful confidence booster. You must have faith in your abilities to accomplish the things that matter the most to you. When you second guess yourself, hesitate and hold back in fear, you are subjecting yourself to a mind of mental torture. You don't deserve that. Self-doubt is a confidence killer, so you should do everything that you can to encourage yourself in the things that matter to you.

- **The more confident you are in yourself, the less easy it will be to succumb to negativity, fear, and self-doubt.** You will in turn enjoy more peace, creativity, and freedom to go after the things that matter the most to you. Self-doubt creates anxiety, depression, and loneliness, whereas confidence creates an abundant flow of possibilities.

- **You will feel powerful and strong:** Wouldn't it be amazing to feel this way in midlife, even when you have those low mood swings? Having full confidence in yourself will leave you feeling invincible at times. That is because your inner power and drive are charged with positivity and maturity. Staying on the path of self-care, self-love, and self-compassion will solidify your confidence in yourself.

- **You will no longer care what others think of you:** Confidence will keep out the negative opinions of others. When you are confident and carefree you will undoubtedly stop caring about what others think of you. Instead, you will care more about what YOU think of YOU. That is exactly as it should be. In your life, you are the most important person. No one wakes up every morning dedicated to your life and everything important to you. It is only YOU who needs to believe in yourself completely and unconditionally.

- **Stress will decrease:** This is one of the best rewards of being confident. You can simply toss aside things that are not important to you, while you prioritize and energize your days with activities that bring you more joy and not stress. You will naturally feel more inclined to avoid stress, and you will feel less anxious about the unknown. You will be more relaxed and comfortable with yourself as well as with others. You will express yourself freely, and not be attached to the consequences of your contribution. Your social engagements will also improve as you totally permit yourself to be your full version without any fear of not being good enough standing in your way.

- **You will have peace of mind:** Since you are happier when you are confident, your life will no longer be riddled with fear, anxiety, and worry. Your life will feel more peaceful as you persist in ensuring that it is. By continuously flipping that switch in your mind from negative to positive and increasing efforts to maintain positivity all day long, in all areas of your life, you will achieve inner peace. (Montano, 2020)

Can you think of anything in your life that is preventing you from experiencing the full benefits of confidence, as mentioned above? What can you do today to invite more confidence back into your life?

_____

_____

_____

_____

_____

_____

_____

_____

_____

_____

_____

_____

_____

_____

38 | *Self-Confidence Workbook for Women*

Factors That Negatively Impact Confidence

There are more people who struggle with confidence than there are those who don't. If you talk to anyone today intimately, you will discover that most people do have personal issues they haven't fully confronted. Low self-confidence leads to inferiority complexes and this in turn creates more self-doubt. Also, while you may be confident in some areas of your life, there may be other areas that require more work.

You most likely discovered this for yourself when you completed the above practical exercise. Below are the most common negative factors that influence a woman's self-confidence. All of the issues listed below can be dissolved, healed, and released, so they no longer have a profound impact on both your self-esteem and self-confidence.

Feeling Like You Have To Be Perfect

As women we know that sometimes we have unreasonably high expectations of ourselves. Perfection is an unrealistic expectation. It is not a defining factor of achieving true success. In midlife especially, we must let go of this false notion. Developing a healthy self-esteem, and a balanced approach to challenges, setbacks, and conflict is more of a winning approach to embracing life in general. The expectation of achieving perfection will inevitably result in a loss of self-confidence. It creates mental pressure and can lead to mental health issues, inferiority complexes, and even eating disorders. The latter occurs especially when body image is impacted by this false notion.

We must accept that no one is perfect, including ourselves. Everyone is on their own journey striving to achieve happiness, success, good health, and personal validation. All of these things can only be attained when we set realistic expectations for ourselves, and practice self-love, self-care, and self-compassion. Embracing imperfection as the norm is the first powerful step you can take to heal your psychological health today. Start letting go of all unrealistic expectations that you have of yourself.

Can you list them here? What are your unrealistic expectations: The ones that create mental pressure when you think, "I absolutely must achieve this now, because if I don't then I will feel more insecure about myself!"

1.	
2.	
3.	
4.	
5.	
6.	
7.	
8.	
9.	
10.	
11.	
12.	
13.	
14.	
15.	
16.	
17.	
18.	
19.	
20.	

Disapproving Authority Figures

Some of us have grown up with disapproving authority figures who have consistently pulled us down in the confidence department. A child needs support, encouragement, and assurance to feel valuable, worthy, and capable. If you grew up in a home environment where the authority figures were not encouraging, supportive, and sensitive about your needs, you most likely grew up feeling insecure, unloved, and unworthy. Childhood authority figures who consistently disapprove of your conduct and who end up being the "negative talk" you had to listen to while growing up, have done some damage to your natural feeling of confidence as a child.

On the other hand, when you are the cause of negative self-talk, it is only a question of deciding to flip the switch in your thoughts from negative to be more supportive, loving, kind, and positive. However, if you've been consistently on the receiving end of negative feedback from authority figures or anyone else, it does require more extensive healing and work on yourself to start building your confidence again. It can be achieved through the practice of self-care. Importantly, giving recognition to the fact that the negative feedback you were subjected to was unfair, unloving, and unsupportive, is just as important. As an adult you must see everything now for what it really was: Emotionally wounded authority figures negating who you were because they didn't know any better themselves at the time.

Childhood Issues and Trauma

If you were impacted in your childhood by trauma or negativity, it can affect you for many years, and lead to much anxiety. Traumatic childhood experiences do still create feelings of inadequacy in adults. It can also lead to ongoing psychological health issues, eating disorders, or any other kind of negative habit. Children need love, nurturing, support, and validation to grow into confident adults who can cope with life's inevitable challenges. When children don't get what they need, to grow up into confident adults, they will struggle to achieve a sense of independence, and personal fulfillment early on in their lives.

As an adult, you may still end up second-guessing yourself not knowing how you truly measure up for love and approval, even when reaching midlife. You may have grown up riddled with worry, and feelings of deep inadequacy, and you may still be carrying some of that energy with you now. Childhood molds a person's beliefs, thoughts, attitudes, and choices in the future. It is therefore a critical part of a person's development. Growing up in abusive, dysfunctional homes can scar a child for life in some instances.

As an adult, if you're still experiencing emotional responses based on your childhood or upbringing it's never too late to reach out to a professional mental health professional to deal with those issues. It is also never too late to begin healing the inner child within, even in midlife. Abuse of any kind leaves psychological wounds that need your attention. You may just need to take time out for yourself to reflect on your childhood, commiserate about those early days, and figure out how some of your childhood challenges may still be impacting your present-day choices.

We must mourn what has passed and look deeper within ourselves to forgive, heal, and let go of those early childhood experiences. It will always remain a fundamental part of your journey, so do not dismiss those memories altogether. Rather learn to reconcile with those memories, lovingly now as you enter the second Spring of your life. Whether it was a good childhood or a semi-good one or an abusive and dysfunctional one, write down how you feel about your childhood, and how it may or may not have impacted your level of confidence. Keep in mind that healing and releasing these memories lovingly will improve your level of confidence in yourself now. Your inner child needs you and your love now to heal the past.

_____

_____

_____

_____

42 | *Self-Confidence Workbook for Women*

Marcee A Martin | **43**

A Negative Work Environment

Another common factor that can create temporary damage to your self-esteem and self-confidence is being exposed to a negative and toxic work environment for an extended period of time. Once again, authority figures in the work environment can wield a lot of power over you, when you allow their negativity to infiltrate your sacred space. The truth of the matter is that some work environments are toxic. The culture of working in teams can be toxic in some instances. The entire work environment can become contaminated with negative vibes, bad attitudes, a lack of integrity, and a host of other issues that make it unhealthy. Working under such conditions can be demoralizing, and unproductive.

If you find yourself being negatively impacted in such a work environment, you must realize that the sooner you leave such an environment the healthier you will become. Negativity is a factor that can easily impact us. Whether we are dealing with double-crossing friends, colleagues, or bosses who lack integrity, the impact is more stress and low self-confidence in this area of your life. The best dose of self-love you can give yourself in this situation is to acknowledge the problem and work towards achieving a long-term career solution.

You must do your best, especially now in midlife to find work that is compelling, inspiring, and fulfilling. Changing jobs or a career entirely is one of the common life-changing decisions that midlifers take. A change in your work environment can end up being as good as taking a vacation when you find the right fit and a supportive work environment. Let's take a moment to think about your career path and work-life history.

How do you feel about your current job? Does the work environment support and recognize your achievements within the organization? Are you settled in this job? Do you have other options that you would like to explore which will boost your level of self-confidence and enthusiasm for your work? Write down your answers below.

Marcee A Martin | **45**

Your Personal Beliefs

Personal beliefs are formed as we progress in life. Every experience we have offers us an opportunity to revisit those beliefs and create new ones. Sadly, most of us have formed negative beliefs about ourselves, and our potential, based on negative past experiences. Some of these beliefs may have become deeply ingrained in your psyche and continue to determine your reactions and outlook on life. Midlife is an amazing time to awaken to new possibilities, examine our belief systems, and toss some of them out. Midlife can be a deeply cleansing and spiritual experience. It is not just biological changes we are going through. Your spirituality can expand during this important transition.

Our personal beliefs also shape our spiritual life. If you have a narrow belief in several important areas of your life, you are most likely not going to excel in those areas. As you open your mind to question limiting beliefs and create new ever expanding ones to support your onward journey, your confidence is also bound to expand and grow. It can grow as vast as the Universe if you permit yourself to change negative beliefs into more empowering ones. I invite you now to examine some of your beliefs here. Ask yourself: Is it allowing you to grow and enjoy new experiences or have these beliefs put up some walls in your life?

Remember the following: Any negative belief will hold you back from experiencing full confidence in yourself!

Example: I am not smart enough and therefore won't be able to excel in my field of profession as others are doing.

Marcee A Martin | 47

Relationships

The quality of your relationships with others may also impact your confidence negatively. If you are enjoying a healthy, trusting, and spiritually rewarding relationship with others, you are most likely going to feel more confident. This applies to all scenarios. Therefore examine the quality of your relationships. Romantic relationships too can be most challenging to your confidence. If you are feeling happy, fulfilled, and supported you are most likely going to experience emotional conflict and this will pull down your level of confidence.

If you've ever experienced a nasty breakup, this could also seriously impact how you measure yourself as being worthy of love. Unless you maturely view the breakup for the quality of your relationship and look at events that may have been beyond your control, you could end up blaming yourself entirely and this experience will undoubtedly result in emotional difficulty for some time to come. Every experience and emotional conflict leaves an energetic imprint on our body, mind, and soul. This is why energetic healing is also gaining in popularity today.

Emotions take up space in our body, and can also manifest into sickness, disease, and chronic stress. You can heal yourself if you are willing to go deeper into some of those past issues, to see that it is no longer relevant. You can work through those emotions with love and respect for the most important person in your life right now: YOU. Keep in mind that even though it is natural to react emotionally to matters of the heart, we don't have to hold onto them for eternity.

Let's check in now, to find out how your relationships with others are impacting your level of self-confidence. List all the important relationships in your life, and examine their quality. Determine for yourself where and how you can increase your level of confidence if some of these relationships are pulling you down. What are some of the unresolved issues in these relationships and are there any patterns emerging that are related to your past relationship experiences?

Marcee A Martin | 49

The Link Between Self-Esteem and Self-Confidence

There is no doubt an important link between self-esteem and self-confidence. How you think and feel about yourself will always impact your self-confidence. Also, how others treat you, respect you, and validate your contribution impacts both self-esteem and self-confidence. However, becoming dependent on external validation should be a contributing factor to how you feel about yourself. It should be, "the cherry on the top!"

Feeling good about yourself starts and ends with you. Developing healthy self-esteem remains an important priority, as this will strengthen your sense of independence, contribution, and confidence. There is nothing wrong with enjoying external validation. However, it should not be your priority or obsession. Win your own approval first, and feel amazing from within.

How Can You Tell if You Have Healthy Self-Esteem?

1. If you avoid dwelling on the past.
2. You don't overthink negative experiences.
3. You regard yourself as being equal to others.
4. You believe in yourself.
5. You don't have a problem expressing your needs.
6. You feel confident in yourself.
7. You have a positive outlook on life.
8. You are not afraid of saying "no" when you need to.
9. You recognize and accept your strengths and weaknesses.

When you have healthy self-esteem, you will experience greater confidence in your life. You will also rise to challenges and face setbacks head-on. A person with healthy self-esteem enjoys life and looks forward to achieving their goals. They are also not afraid of failure or exploring new opportunities. (Cherry, 2022)

50 | *Self-Confidence Workbook for Women*

How Does Low Self-Esteem Manifest in Your Life?

1. You compare yourself to others frequently.
2. You always see others as being better than you.
3. You struggle to express your needs.
4. You tend to put others on a pedestal.
5. You see yourself as being beneath others.
6. You focus more on your weaknesses.
7. You tend to avoid socializing with others.
8. You have a negative outlook on life.
9. You are more afraid of failure than you are willing to try something new.
10. You find it difficult to accept positive feedback about yourself.
11. You have trouble saying "no" to people.
12. You are more of a people pleaser.
13. You put other people's needs above your own.
14. You find it difficult to set healthy boundaries for yourself.
15. You avoid confrontations at all costs.
16. You lack confidence in yourself and your abilities.

Low self-esteem will impact all areas of your life negatively. You will feel drained, and unmotivated and will not be able to progress easily. Unless you shift your mindset you may also experience mental health issues. The overall quality of your life will depreciate and your self-confidence will dwindle day by day. Seeking professional help might be your best option to receive support in your journey to fully regain self-confidence. (Cherry, 2022)

Excessive Self-Esteem Is Not Healthy

This might come as a surprise to you, but excessive self-confidence may be unhealthy in some instances. It may be a sign of narcissism, which is a personality disorder that requires the help of a mental health professional. Overconfidence may also be indicative of a fragile ego, making up for perceived inadequacies. In other words, it is a cover-up! Anyone displaying excessive self-esteem or confidence will most likely fit this profile below:

1. You are preoccupied with perfection.
2. You want to be the center of attention to feel good about yourself.
3. You may hate failure, and crumble at the thought of it.
4. You like putting on a show to get everyone's attention, and to soothe your fragile ego.
5. You may express grandiose ideas in every situation, to receive excess attention.
6. You may grossly overestimate your abilities.

A person who displays the above is draining to be around. Always the attention seeker is bound to drive people away from you if they get close enough. Narcissism can be charming at first but it will destroy the self-esteem of others in your life who get too close to you. It is not confidence, but a display of a very wounded ego. Narcissism requires professional treatment to get back to being psychologically healthy, and empathetic. (Cherry, 2022)

Here's How You Can Improve Your Self-Esteem

1. Flip your internal dialogue from negative to positive.
2. Stop comparing yourself to others.
3. Count your blessings.
4. Do not rely on external validation to feel good about yourself.
5. Be your own champion by setting goals and achieving them.
6. Identify distorted thoughts that may be negatively impacting your psychological health.
7. Challenge your negative behavior as they show up in your life.
8. Use positive affirmations daily to keep yourself feeling inspired.
9. Practice self-love, self-care, and self-compassion more often.

52 | *Self-Confidence Workbook for Women*

Can you identify with healthy, low, or excessive self-esteem in your behavior? What are some of the distorted ideas you have about yourself that need to be rectified?

Key Takeaways

- Most of us have experienced low levels of confidence under very challenging circumstances in our lives.
- Our past can haunt us for many years unless we change that!
- We cannot change the past but we can heal it.
- Self-confidence will bring you more success and happiness in life.
- Self-confidence will decrease self-doubt.
- You will be able to make stronger choices and better decisions for your life, with confidence.
- Confidence removes the fear factor in all situations.
- When you are confident in yourself and your abilities you can live life on your own terms!
- When you are confident you will feel powerful and strong!
- When you are confident you will no longer care what other people think of you!
- Enjoying healthier relationships with healthy boundaries in place is a sign of confidence.
- When you are confident you will feel great in your skin and won't compare yourself to others.
- A confident person recognizes that negative thinking is a waste of precious energy and time.
- You will get on with your goals, feeling inspired from within, when you are confident in yourself.

In the next inspiring chapter, we will work on developing your mindset to support building more confidence. You must become unstoppable!

CHAPTER 3

SETTING UP THE RIGHT MINDSET FOR THE BEST FOOT FORWARD

Midlife calls to every woman to develop themselves in new ways, and to open up more like a flower in full bloom revealing her beauty. –Marcee A Martin

The Natural Success Mindset

You may be familiar with what low confidence feels like. For me, it's a squirmy feeling in the pit of my tummy. In the past, I had no confidence when it came to expressing my ideas. It felt like a hole in the earth had opened up to swallow me up, whenever I had to speak in public. I cringed at the thought of making a fool of myself and secretly cried at the shame I felt for having those deep feelings of inadequacy. Low confidence is a defeatist attitude that we display about ourselves to the world, and it is also often a self-fulfilling prophecy. It calls to you when you are in short supply of it, by feelings of physical discomfort. You also intrinsically know that you lack confidence when you compare yourself to others, and when you keep bringing yourself down.

Do you recall the last time you wished you had the shape of someone else's body or the success they enjoyed when you compare yourself to them? We are sometimes all guilty of doing this: Comparing ourselves to others! It is an unhealthy habit that will keep you away from adopting a natural success mindset. How often do you compare yourself to someone else? What do you feel is lacking in your life right now?

The foundation of a natural success mindset is to first recognize your strengths and talents. Once you do this, you can then take inspiring action to achieve great results with those unique strengths and talents. When you do this, it builds confidence in YOU. A natural success mindset includes embracing every area of your life in a way that supports its development. A natural success mindset embraces the idea of living your best life today, to enjoy high-quality results in every area of your life.

If you lack confidence, you are bound to make more mistakes, second guess your life, and stumble. You will undoubtedly miss many wonderful opportunities that come your way. Not believing in yourself holds us back more than we even care to admit. It would be painful to recall how you held back from exploring new opportunities because of lacking confidence. However, when we do so, we can open our minds and hearts to see that we have it in us to shift from this feeling of lack to abundance!

Marcee A Martin | **57**

Can you recall some of the times in your life when you did not pursue opportunities because you were lacking in self-confidence? It's never too late to change that.

When I reached midlife I felt more deserving of regaining my confidence. There was a time in my life when I struggled intensely with psychological and emotional issues. I suffered from chronic anxiety, low self-confidence, and other emotional disorders that left me spiraling into a dark place. Low self-confidence brings on a plethora of psychological issues that negatively impact every area of your life. Thankfully, when I reached midlife I experienced a great awakening and made a new, empowering choice. I wanted to feel more deserving of success and went all out to learn how to achieve this.

Feeling Deserving of Success

If you find yourself in the boat of feeling less deserving of success, then take comfort in the fact that everything is reversible. We've all been in that boat! Therefore, in midlife, you owe it to yourself to experience a newfound sense of freedom and confidence. Ultimately having high confidence includes feeling deserving of success. It also includes a willingness to liberate yourself from all of the past issues that may have held you back in life. There is only one person who needs to feel inherently worthy of success. That one person is YOU.

Setting things right from within is key to overcoming anxiety, negativity, and self-doubt. Achieving confidence and success is an inside job more than it is an outside job. That means you must shift your mental attitude and beliefs about success from within, to experience higher levels of self-deserve. So what can you do today to start developing a healthy, and natural success mindset, that includes feeling more deserving? Here are some important tips to get you on that successful thinking trajectory. It does require more conscious action on your part.

Tips for Building a Positively Successful Mindset

Growth Mindset Versus Fixed Mindset

There are two mindsets that influence your ability to grow and succeed. If you follow a growth mindset outlook, then your chances of succeeding, and experiencing healthy self-confidence are stronger. The growth mindset involves embracing more opportunities to support personal development and growth. When you are influenced by this outlook, you will naturally be more inclined to embrace both challenge and opportunity. You will also not be deeply affected by moments of failure or setbacks. You will strive to see everything as being on the way and not in the way. You will believe in your ability to adapt and change as life dictates.

On the other hand, someone who approaches life with a fixed mind tends to be less flexible, and less adaptable to change. They also struggle more with challenges and view them as obstacles, internalizing failure

60 | *Self-Confidence Workbook for Women*

as a reflection of their limiting abilities. People with a fixed mindset also quit easily when the going gets tough. They believe in luck instead of hard work and usually don't take active steps to improve their lives in the face of challenges.

This is why it is important to be aware of how your brain can support your development. When you focus on results and bypass the fixed outlook, as well as deeply ingrained negative habits, you will start experiencing more growth and you will be more open and willing to take active steps to rewire your brain with new habits. Here's how you can accomplish moving away from a fixed mindset to a more growth-oriented mindset:

1. Believe in your abilities.
2. Learn new skills by adopting a plan that supports your growth consistently.
3. Avoid internalizing failure as a fault of yours. Instead, see failure as experience.
4. See effort as being key to transforming your life and tipping the scales of success more in your favor.
5. Make the effort to get the results you desire.
6. Be more resilient when facing adversity.
7. Take on a "can do" approach.
8. Avoid falling into the trap of feeling hopeless. Get up and keep moving forward toward your goals.
9. Be open to trying new ways and approaches to challenges.
10. Find new solutions, by making new resolutions and setting healthy boundaries to support your growth.
11. Make yourself and your goals a priority in your life.
12. Be flexible in your approach to change.
13. Be on the lookout for new creative opportunities to expand your interest and enthusiasm.

Improve Emotional Intelligence

Managing your emotions in difficult situations is better overall for your psychological health and wellness. If you allow painful emotions to fester and build momentum, it can lead to stress, anxiety, and low confidence in yourself. When you are facing strong emotions, press pause, take a step back to view the situation objectively, and come up with a less emotional approach. It is important to deal with your emotions, especially during midlife when this transition is also characterized by mood swings, emotional discomfort, and hormonal imbalance. Practice the following tips to strengthen your emotional intelligence:

1. Pay attention to your emotions regularly.

2. Notice the triggers and the underlying issues.

3. Try to maintain equilibrium and communicate your feelings maturely, without negating yourself or others.

4. Address the issue and use emotion as a sign that something needs your attention.

5. Remember that emotions may arise from any unknown source of frustration.

6. Take a deep breath and assess any potential damage you could do to a situation if you leave your emotions unchecked.

7. Be open to listening to others, to obtain their feedback during the conflict.

8. Be willing to achieve mutually acceptable solutions.

9. Value diversity in perspective and opinions.

10. Consider the consequences of your actions.

11. Always put your best foot forward believing in your ability to rise above strong emotions.

12. Focus more on positive emotions, and amplify them!

13. Practice more self-care and self-compassion during emotionally challenging times.

14. Do not ignore your feelings altogether.

15. Honor your emotions by allowing them to show you the way to the source of your discomfort. Awareness leads to the discovery of more long-term solutions.

Strengthen Your Willpower

Willpower is the elixir to staying on your path of growth! Whenever we are making inroads to achieve greater success in our lives, we need staying power to stick with the plan! We've all been on diets in the past to lose weight, so we know that we need willpower and motivation to keep going, to see the results manifest in front of our eyes. The magic ingredient in any successful formula is willpower. When the going gets tough, your willpower and determination will determine how strong you are to keep you on the path to your success. Here's how you can do that:

1. Set small incremental goals to reach the target.
2. Celebrate the milestones as you progress.
3. Keep a journal to check in daily.
4. Report back on your efforts each and every day in your journal.
5. Hold yourself accountable when you slip up.
6. Highlight your reasons, then get back up on that horse of willpower!
7. Reward yourself when you achieve small goals.
8. Remember that all steps add up in the long run.
9. Remind yourself every day why achieving your goals is important to you.
10. Use positive affirmations and self-compassion to talk yourself through all setbacks and challenges.
11. Don't give up on yourself when things get tough.
12. Double up for lost time and stick to deadlines!
13. Stay curious and keep learning new things to challenge yourself.
14. Always set the bar higher as you progress, it will strengthen your willpower, and motivate you!

15. Don't allow competition to scare you away. Look ahead and focus on your personal goals that define success for you as an individual. (Cherry, 2022)

Can you identify areas listed above for improvement that will enhance your self-confidence further? What came up for you personally as you read through the lists above? Identifying areas of improvement will give you a clear indication of what you can do to improve your behavior, attitude, and beliefs.

Marcee A Martin | **65**

Winning the Battle for Control of Your Mind

One of the most significant battles we face during this important midlife transition is facing our inner demons. Others refer to this as dealing with our darker sides. These sides reflect unresolved past issues, or mental challenges that interrupt a more natural flow of happiness, wellness, peace, and success! In midlife, everything seems more intense. Transitions are always uncomfortable, but getting to a better mental state is achievable. As long as you remain consciously aware of what is going on inside of you, and deal with it head-on, there is no reason why you will stay stuck in negativity.

Controlling Intrusive Thoughts

It may be harder on some days than others to get past the controlling intrusive thoughts that come up for you in midlife. This is why journaling remains an important part of your ongoing healing journey. The greater your commitment to healing, the greater your chances are of overcoming intrusive thoughts as they appear in your life. Your mind should be your personal sanctuary for positivity, inspiration, and growth. Your attention should focus on planting those seeds instead of harboring negative feelings.

These controlling intrusive thoughts are the red flags letting you know that it may be time to let go of something in your life that has been bringing you down for a long time. Any intrusive thoughts that result in you not feeling good about yourself must be vanquished. It might seem easier said than done. However, it is achievable if you are patient with yourself and don't give up.

For example, if you've had a negative experience with someone who has pulled you down, and you discover that re-engagement with them has caused the same negative intrusive thoughts from the past to reappear, then it's time to heal those negative thoughts in a way that will help you to let go of the past. A solution may be to clear up the old issues with them directly or to re-examine new resolutions to avoid a repeat of a bad experience with them.

You may also want to limit your time with them until you can fully heal and let go of those residual feelings that have re-emerged in your mind. It is important to recognize that in midlife you could have many intrusive controlling thoughts emerging in your mind that need your attention. There will, however, always be the dominant ones that tend to interfere with how you feel, your level of productivity, and how you react to situations that trigger more of those dark thoughts. Here's how you can handle it when it shows up for you:

Write down the dominant intrusive thoughts that come up for you, which results in lower self-esteem and lower self-confidence.

For example: Whenever I think of an experience I feel deeply insecure about myself. It is the hurt and pain of this situation that brings me down and interrupts my natural enthusiasm and confidence.

68 | *Self-Confidence Workbook for Women*

Now ask yourself how you could adequately resolve that issue. What would bring you peace? Avoidance might work only in the short term. You need to be very specific about the solutions that feel right for you. Take some time out now to meditate on the situation, to come to solutions that feel right from within. When you are ready, write them down here.

Your aim must be to break free completely from the clutches of these negative thoughts. Remember: Nothing should have power over your peace of mind. How you feel about yourself is truly important. Be your own best friend and fight for yourself in your mind by acknowledging intrusive thoughts for what they are: Unresolved Issues that need to be healed and released! Are you ready to break free from those intrusive thoughts?

What would you like to be free of to experience more joy and less regret?

Marcee A Martin | 71

Keep This In Mind About Midlife

You will feel tension, and conflict as you transition through midlife. What worked in the past may no longer work for you in various areas of your life at present. The midlife spiritual awakening does bring tension and change as you realize that your clock is clicking! This is what awakens most women in midlife to explore new dreams and goals. The idea is to work towards fully embracing your midlife years with a renewed sense of hope and confidence. Follow these inspiring tips to bring you back into balance and to keep your energy flowing naturally and with ease.

- **Don't ignore the changes in your body:** Adjust your diet accordingly to bring new vitality, and health to your life. Embrace the midlife version of yourself with all the changes underway. Creating a new lifestyle and self-care routine is a marvelous way of honoring these changes occurring now in your body and in your mind.

- **Don't put limits on your life:** Go ahead and explore new opportunities. Pull out the stops and set down to achieving your midlife goals, one step at a time! Start your day off with an inspiring morning routine, and fill your day up with inspiring activities that are meaningful and rewarding to you.

- **Explore your individual beliefs as well as your cultural beliefs about getting older below:** Ask yourself what are your cultural expectations, and how do these, together with your personal beliefs about midlife shape your new current reality?

Marcee A Martin | 73

- **Explore yourself:** Remember that since you are going through changes, it is important to continue with your healing journey to trace your footsteps. Explore your new beliefs, likes, dislikes, and expectations for yourself. Having expectations is a sign of enthusiasm, and it will give you the confidence you need to stay on the path of your inspiring midlife journey. (Kirilova, 2019)

Some of the questions you can ask yourself may include the following:

1. Who is the person you are becoming?
2. What do you want in life?
3. How can you improve your life in all areas with hindsight?
4. When you look in the mirror what do you see in yourself?
5. Are you able to pursue your dreams more confidently now?
6. What values do you need to project about yourself that align you with all that is important to you in life?

74 | *Self-Confidence Workbook for Women*

Marcee A Martin | 75

Here's an important question to consider now that you are gaining more clarity about the direction you would like your life to take: **What are you doing now at present to create the next chapter of your life?**

Becoming Unstoppable

Becoming unstoppable is what will happen when you regain full confidence in yourself. If you have experienced a midlife slump and are still feeling slightly despondent about what your chances are of "making it at midlife," here are some powerful tips to follow that will take you on the path of becoming unstoppable:

1. **Follow your true purpose:** Whatever ignites your inner flame, is what gives you a sense of purpose. Don't hesitate to start following that purpose today, by exploring ways that you can manifest it. There may be several different paths that lead you to feel purposeful. It doesn't have to just be one thing. For example, you may want to explore entrepreneurial opportunities, while also nurturing a hobby as an extra creative outlet. Or you may want to volunteer your time to a social cause of your choice.

2. **Believe in yourself and your ideas:** Every great change in the world, regardless of its magnitude, is a service that you are offering to others. Don't be afraid of those ideas that call to you. Believe in yourself, and take strategic and purposeful action today to move in the direction of your new ideas! Every great entrepreneur is successful because they believe in their ideas. They were also willing to give it their best shot! Everything starts with belief. Let it power you up, to keep you moving in the pursuit of your ideas.

3. **Be prepared for challenges and setbacks:** Every new idea that you pursue will come with its own unique set of challenges. Don't let that stop you. Set your path on fire with determination, resilience, and passion! Life is a mixed bag of blessings. See everything as being on the way, and not in the way. When something doesn't work out it usually leaves a trace of wisdom in its path for you to explore. New ideas always emerge to replace the old ones. Welcome the challenge as your old friend, instead of cursing the darkness.

4. **Don't be afraid to ask for help:** Connect with like-minded people on your path, and share ideas. Reach out to them for help, and

build a strong support network that will further strengthen your development and growth. The more you connect with your support network, the more you will grow personally, and professionally.

5. **Seek out creative, innovative solutions:** For every challenge, setback, or problem, there is always a solution waiting to be discovered. This is what makes the journey all the more interesting. Be innovative in your quest to come up with new creative solutions. Being unstoppable means setting yourself up to succeed. What that picture of success looks like to you in your mind's eye should be motivation enough to keep you moving forward, to expand, grow and innovate! Persevere, no matter what the challenges are.

6. **Never give up on yourself:** Giving up is not an option for anyone who is unstoppable! Never, never, never, give up on yourself! The journey will make you stronger, wiser, and more knowledgeable. Even when the going gets tough, just refuse to give up. Take a break, relax, and unwind to ensure that the stress does not turn into a negative belief! Just keep going forward, even if it is baby steps that you're taking. Eventually, you will reach your destination. (Grant, 2013)

Quick journal check-in: How do you feel about becoming unstoppable?

78 | *Self-Confidence Workbook for Women*

Worksheet for Improving Your Mindset

Mental Exercises To Train Your Mind To Become Unstoppable!

Remind yourself of these mental power-thinking habits every morning and evening to raise your level of confidence and stay connected to adopting a powerful new thinking pattern.

1.	Choose to live your life on your terms.	Stick to your high-priority activities and complete them. Prioritize your life according to what is important to you!
2.	Don't be afraid of failure.	If you fail, make adjustments and keep moving forward!

3.	Don't compete with others.	Stick to your goals, and focus on honing your own skills and competencies. Be Unique and be impeccable in your efforts!
4.	Never stop learning.	Learn something new every day in your field of interest! It will keep you inspired, and result in further growth and improvements.
5.	Own your own space.	Hold yourself accountable for excellence. When you make mistakes, own them. When you achieve your goals, celebrate them!
6.	Purge all things that are negative in your life.	Get rid of negativity daily in your thoughts and actions! Surround yourself with inspiration.
7.	Never settle for less than you deserve.	Keep your cup flowing with inspirational ideas, and power up your expectations! Keep raising the bar!
8.	Build up your mental strength daily.	Pressure builds your mental stamina, so don't succumb to it! Focus on the end goal, and remember why it is important to you.
9.	Remember that your confidence is your greatest asset.	To achieve great things you must have great confidence in yourself.
10.	Let things go!	Be willing to forgive and move on graciously when things get tough! Also be willing to let people go from your life, if necessary. Don't hold on to negative, emotional baggage.

Mindfulness Practice

To improve our mental and emotional well-being it is important to create a mindfulness culture daily. This will carry you through any challenging day and improve your mind-body balance. All you need is a few moments during the day to achieve calm, and peace in between your busy schedule. Do your best to achieve this daily and you will reap the rewards (James, 2017).

Practice Mindfulness Breathing Daily To Relax, Unwind, and Release Negativity

This exercise is a powerful neutralizer. You can do it as follows, either standing or sitting on a chair or comfortably on the floor in the lotus position, used for meditation. Start with ten minutes and increase the exercise if needed.

1. Sit comfortably and allow your body to relax.
2. Consciously allow all your thoughts, worries, or emotions to leave your body.
3. Start by breathing in and out slowly.
4. Consciously release negativity and anything uncomfortable.
5. Breathe gently through your nose and exhale through your mouth.
6. Just consciously keep letting go of your thoughts and anything else that comes up for you.
7. Become one with your breath.
8. Scan your body slowly moving up from your feet until you reach the crown of your head.
9. As you do this, become aware of any sensations in your body.
10. Ensure that you are completely relaxed, and feeling calmer in body, mind, and spirit.
11. Once you are ready you can go on with your day's activities.

Yoga and Meditation

Use yoga daily and meditation to stay connected to your body, mind, and soul. The benefits of sticking to a yoga routine in the mornings or evenings are a powerful way to reflect on the day ahead and unwind completely in the evenings. Keep it simple when you begin and expand on the routine as you progress.

Start or End Your Day With Yoga Followed by Meditation

1. Choose a simple 10 to 20-minute yoga session online by searching for a suitable morning or evening yoga session on YouTube.
2. You don't need to study yoga, but just give it a shot to experience how it makes you feel if you are just starting.
3. If you prefer to start with a mindfulness breathing meditation before the yoga session you may do so, or you can end the yoga session with the meditation.
4. Wear comfortable clothing and use a yoga mat.
5. Drink a glass of water before the session, or you can sip water in between.
6. Follow through from start to finish, and add on a three-minute silent peace meditation at the end.
7. Breath in gently through your nose and out through your mouth.
8. Consciously send peace and love to every cell in your body.
9. Imagine a white light surrounding your body, and allow peace to enter your space.
10. Thereafter imagine the planet, and send peace and love to all living beings on the planet.
11. Finally picture the earth in your mind's eye, as if you are viewing it from outer-space and send peace and love to the entire Universe.
12. Stretch your hands up and outwards to the Universe and expand your energy upwards and outwards.

82 | *Self-Confidence Workbook for Women*

Getting Into Shape

Getting in shape will have many benefits for you as a midlife woman (Perry, 2010).

1. It reduces the negative side effects of hormonal imbalance.

2. Exercise will help you stay healthy, feel good, and keep the excess weight off.

3. Reduces hot and cold flashes.

4. You will feel more energized and motivated to feel good about yourself.

5. Exercise reduces stress, and helps you energize for your tasks ahead.

6. It will also reduce intense mood swings: Another midlife side effect of hormonal changes.

7. Reduces the risk of heart disease, and other medical conditions, more so if you follow a healthy eating diet.

8. Exercise will reduce cholesterol in the body, and your bloodstream.

9. Reduces anxiety and depression.

10. Strengthens your immune system.

11. Improves your focus, and enhances mental clarity.

Creating Healthy Daily Habits

Finally, here are some additional power tips to help you to succeed each and every day in your life. It is yet another one of my magic formulas that helps me stay on my path of confidence, success, and happiness!

1. Ensure that you are developing good habits to replace ones that are having a toxic impact on your life.

2. Getting important rest in the evenings after your yoga and meditation session is essential.

3. Make sure that your daily healthy habit includes adjusting your schedule to maintain a healthy, vibrant self-care routine.

4. Take care of all your top priorities each day before anything else!

5. To be unstoppable you must manage your time effectively.

6. Cut out unnecessary low-priority distractions.

7. Make space to spend quality time with those you love!

8. Surround yourself with inspiration!

9. Keep your positive levels up consistently!

10. Do what you love, and love what you do!

In the next Chapter, we will root out the dark programming that keeps us playing small!

CHAPTER 4:

REMOVING THE DARK SIDE: HOW TO REMOVE THE BAD PROGRAMMING INSIDE YOUR MIND

A strong, confident woman is aware of her own strengths, value, and worth. –Marcee A Martin.

Understanding Your Potential

If you are anything like how I was in the past, then you were also most likely once a people pleaser! As women, we do tend to be guilty of not wanting to rock the boat (mess things up) in tense situations and in general. The socialized expectation is to be well-behaved women, as caregivers and nurturers. As a woman, I found that I have not expressed my needs enough in the past, both to myself and others, in situations that warranted free expression. Thankfully, midlife changes that for us. The hormonal changes occurring in our bodies also naturally entice us to throw things out of the window that isn't working for us, including old beliefs, and behavior patterns. As research indicates, we are not as alone in our midlife journey as we think we are.

Women tend to become feistier during these years. The realization that we still have many healthy, inspiring years ahead of us leads to a new awakening in midlife. Taking stock of who we are is a natural occurrence when we reach our late forties. I found that the closer women get to their 50s the more liberating and empowering our journey does become.

Let's pause to ask ourselves: How often do you clearly express your needs to others? What held you back from expressing your needs wholeheartedly, unashamedly, and without a care in the world in the past? It is important to reflect on this. It will help you get to the root cause of some of your insecurities, so that you may heal them.

Having reached midlife, I have realized that I did waste a lot of time trying to fit in, to conform to everyone else's expectations of me in both my personal and professional life. Those choices disempowered me in many ways, pulled me down psychologically, and robbed me of true innovative creativity, as well as personal fulfillment. When I reached midlife I was done with all of that, including the bullshit associated with socialized expectations that women have to meet—to be liked, admired, and appreciated. Being a high-value woman today includes not meeting anyone else's expectations. The objective is to live my life according to my highest values.

That's the beauty of reaching midlife: We can own our individuality, and rock it! At 50 we are clearly not done, and we begin to start reaching within to fully explore our true potential. I feel that most women tend to fully mature by the time they reach 50. At this age, we can begin to explore our true worth and value, while learning from past mistakes. Today, I am one of those strong, powerful women who values and respects herself completely.

It doesn't make me a narcissist or less empathetic. On the contrary, it makes me more empathetic, and more accountable for my own happiness and those who I genuinely love and care about. I've had my own journey of negativity to contend with for many years. Deciding to flip the internal switch in my mind from negative to positive continues to make all the difference in my life.

Quick question: What is the ideal version of yourself that you wish to manifest during your midlife years and why?

Another important discovery I made as I reached midlife is that I wasted too much time in the past mulling over ridiculous things that didn't matter at all. Everyone else's opinion of me no longer matters. It never should've mattered. Being a woman of character, strength, and high value, now in midlife, has opened my mind to new possibilities for growth and development. I have learned to appreciate this famous wise quote often made by Dr. John Demartini, a world-renowned human behavior specialist: "When the vision on the inside is louder than all opinions on the outside then you have truly begun to master your life!" I am confident enough now to draw my line in the sand when necessary these days.

The Midlife Reflection

Midlife is about self-reflection, to heal the shadow parts of ourselves. Those parts in us represent the incorrect perceptions we've held about ourselves over many years. These often distorted, negative perceptions have kept us away from really exploring our full potential. By the time we get to 50, we start awakening to new ideas, and we also start setting the stage to go after the life we deserve to have. By all means, do go after what you want.

I have discovered that once we fully embrace the dark sides of our past, without judgment we can also start accepting the true imperfect nature of life. Once we accept that life and reality will always be flawed, we can start relaxing and mellowing, comforted by the real authentic value of our journey thus far. Accepting the imperfect nature of life is liberating. There is no more pressure to expect perfection, and therefore no reason to submit the limited belief that we are just not good enough. You are enough! Let your cup be filled with inspiration daily, instead of unrealistic expectations of yourself.

Becoming more confident in ourselves includes how we process our life experiences by removing those negative labels we've attached to some of them. We must get rid of those incorrect, often distorted labels. We must also get rid of the dark side of our minds. It is not only the negative thinking that keeps us stuck but it is also the unrealistic fantasized expectations of our lives versus what it is. What it is may exceed our expectations at times, if we choose to appreciate, even the little blessings, and marvel at how far we've come. Sometimes we distort the view of our life experiences, especially when we view things as being inadequate when compared to idealized expectations.

Mundane situations may also present great potential if we start viewing them that way. A badass woman is capable of turning any mundane situation into an unbelievable adventure! At midlife, we can still play, be optimistic, and be adventurous, and we most certainly do stand a better chance of having things go our own way. When you permit yourself to let things go your way, there is no longer a need to attach negative labels to anything that doesn't conform to someone else's expectations or idealized notions of what is better for you. A confident badass midlife woman will do everything possible to enjoy more things working in her favor. There is nothing selfish about this. It is our natural birthright to claim our own happiness. Stick this label around your home and office and remember to always go after what YOU want and value in life.

What Do I Want in Life?

Compile your bucket list now: Make a bucket list of all the things you would love to experience in the next ten years of your life.

1.	
2.	
3.	
4.	
5.	
6.	
7.	
8.	
9.	
10.	
11.	
12.	
13.	
14.	
15.	
16.	

17.	
18.	
19.	
20.	
21.	
22.	
23.	
24.	
25.	
26.	
27.	
28.	
29.	
30.	
31.	
32.	
33.	
34.	
35.	
36.	
37.	
38.	
39.	
40.	

The Golden Rule

The golden rule in life has always been to treat others as you want them to treat you. However, everyone treats others as they feel they deserve to be treated. In other words, we teach others how we would love to be treated. If you find yourself constantly sucking things up that you disapprove of, just because you don't want to be labeled as being a badass then you will constantly be on the receiving end of those things you despise. However, if you show up confidently, instead of being apologetically meek, then there is less likelihood of anyone treating you in a manner that you disapprove of.

Being nice is not necessarily always the right thing to do in all situations, especially when your personal value is at stake. Being a badass in situations that warrants your strong disapproval and rebuke, is appropriate when you need to teach others what is acceptable to you as a high-worth woman, and what is not acceptable to you. These things must reflect YOUR own standards. I bet that these standards are quite high, yet if you are anything like me, we have failed to live by many of them in the past.

When you live by the high standards you've set for yourself it will translate into happiness, when you meet these standards. Also, recognize that: We do and must make adjustments as we go along in life. Recognize the fantasies that you've held onto in the past that created more frustration than happiness for you, versus the new standards and expectations you now live by.

Ask yourself: What are some of the high standards you have in mind to increase your value as a woman today? Did you always live by these standards, and if you compromised on these standards, why do they feel right to you now?

94 | Self-Confidence Workbook for Women

The Destructive Emotional Baggage

Looking deeply at the destructive nature of the negative thoughts, emotions, beliefs, and cycles of repetition that have occurred in our lives to keep us stuck will be deeply insightful. We already know that our thoughts are interchangeable. This means that we can easily shift our thoughts from negative to being more kind, loving, positive, and creative. Our thoughts and feelings are always changeable based on what we are telling ourselves. This means that we can also undo them accordingly and this will lead to more positively inspiring results in our lives. The first part of this journey is to learn how to reduce negative emotions. Let's dive further into this deeply insightful exercise.

Reducing Negative Emotions

Earlier, in Chapter 1, we discussed the brain and how we can use it to rewire our thinking patterns. The neuroplastic nature of the brain allows us to create ongoing new realities for ourselves. The more we repeat this behavior and reinforce it with new healthier habits the greater the momentum will be. Also, the rewiring of new beliefs and habits will occur in your subconscious mind. Eventually, it will become your new approach and it will undoubtedly manifest in greater changes that will take place in your life. This is why it is crucial to commit to changing your thinking patterns regularly especially when you are confronting thoughts that lead you to experience more negative emotions.

Whenever a negative thought about yourself emerges, flip that switch immediately from being negative to positive. Soon it will become a natural habit, and you won't find yourself being constantly in effect by your thoughts. Negative emotions that emerge as a result of your thoughts will make you feel more vulnerable. Any time that you decide to tap into them, you can. All of us in our youth made choices we are not proud of today. However, even those choices must be honored for what it is, and how they shaped our life.

Most women do experience strong emotional reactions to their past upon reflection. In many instances, it is skewed. We look at the negative

Marcee A Martin | 95

impact only, and not at how it has made us wiser. Those were the lessons we needed to learn. On some subconscious level, we chose to have those experiences, and if we didn't we decided how to react to them, and we can still choose how those incidents make us feel today. We are still learning new lessons every day, about ourselves, others, and the world at large. The learning opportunity is endless. It occurs when we begin to make sense of things in our life, and all around us. To experience a new outcome, we can also choose to honor the lessons, instead of condemning ourselves. Here's what you can do to achieve release, and limit the impact of negative emotions in your life:

- **Use mindfulness to combat its impact on you:** Practice mindfulness by asserting yourself as an objective observer. This will help you gain a better handle on any situation. It will also help you to gain a deeper insight into the emotions attached to those experiences. Practice mindfulness with all of your thoughts, allowing them to pass through objectively. Observe them, and take note of why they come up for you.

- **Identify negative thoughts:** Simply take note of the thoughts that are causing negative emotions. Then go deeper to question why those negative thoughts have emerged and why they are appearing in your mind. Always remember that you can simply change the negative thought and the associated emotion attached to it.

- **Replace negative thoughts with more realistic ones:** Choose to hold more appropriate thoughts and delete the negative ones. Place yourself at the center of the new thoughts, as being most worthy of good, loving experiences in life. Avoid jumping to conclusions, based on cognitive distortions that are taking place in your mind due to persistent negative thoughts.

- **Practice acceptance:** When you are dealing with challenging emotions linked to negative experiences, choose acceptance as the preferred outcome. You cannot change the past, but you can choose to accept it for whatever it is. Accept the reality of any situation with self-love, and self-compassion.

96 | *Self-Confidence Workbook for Women*

- **Learning to cope with criticism and feedback:** Life is a balance of support, and challenge. There will be people who love and support you, and those who won't. Think of times when you were critical of others, and unfairly rejected them. Do keep an open mind about all feedback coming your way by practicing mindfulness. You will find a more detailed discussion on criticism in the first book of this series, titled, *The Self Love Workbook For Midlife Women: A 30-Day Healing Journal: Release Toxicity, Overcome Self-Doubt.* (Cuncic, 2023)

People Pleasing Cancer

If you still find yourself striving to please others, just to be accepted, to fit in, or make an impression, it is time to cure yourself of this need. It is okay and healthy to have wonderful, supportive relationships with others. However, it becomes unnatural, forced, and fake when you aim to please others. Everyone lives according to their own set of values and priorities, and if you are not balanced in your approach to people, you could be easily taken advantage of.

You may also be undermining yourself in the process of pleasing others, without realizing it. Aim to put people that you care about in your heart without patronizing them to win their approval. Always avoid placing anyone on a pedestal. Doing this will inflate their worth while minimizing yours. There must be equity in all relationships. Aim to spread your uniqueness in the world without any desire of going out of your way to please others. Be natural.

There is another word that can be ascribed to the tendency of wanting to go out of your way to please others. That word is "co-dependency." It refers to anyone who has low self-esteem, low confidence, and low self-worth, according to their perception. A codependent is a person who is emotionally wounded, and this explains the strong tendency of being a people-pleaser. If you are a codependent whose happiness depends on making others happy, regardless of how they treat you, it is nothing to be ashamed of. You can get help from a professional mental health therapist to get to the root cause of your codependency.

Marcee A Martin | **97**

Contemplate: Do you experience any strain in your current relationships with others but are too afraid to express your true feelings? Can you identify those relationships here, and highlight any issues that you're avoiding bringing up, just to keep up a people-pleasing approach instead?

_____

_____

_____

_____

_____

_____

The Unhealthy Side of Codependency

A codependent's need to serve others is like a people-pleasing obsession. The only way that codependents can feel good about themselves is when they receive the love and approval of others. A codependent behaves like an addict. They are desperate to be loved and therefore become easy victims of those who want to take advantage of their kind nature. Codependents often end up in very abusive relationships. This is largely due to their people-pleasing behavior and being quick to accept blame for everything going wrong in their relationships, even when they are a victim of abuse.

A codependent's need to please often stems from a troubled childhood during which they were not validated, blamed, or abused verbally, physically, or emotionally by their caregivers. Therefore, they grew up needy for love, and approval and always blame themselves when things get tough in relationships. Below is a list of the signs of codependency (Lawrenz, 2022):

1. Minimizes their own needs.

2. Prefer to make other people happy, rather than themselves.

3. They apologize often and blame themselves when things go wrong.

4. They cannot accept compliments easily as they do not believe in themselves.

5. Their moods depend on the moods of others.

6. Displays low self-esteem and low self-confidence.

7. Raise others on pedestals to idolize or worship.

8. They feel guilty when they do things for themselves.

9. They care mainly about what others think of them, and very little about what they think of themselves.

If you identify with any of these traits, the exercises here will help you to develop better faith in yourself. You also might want to consider doing things more on your own, by identifying all the things that you love doing. Then start executing those things according to your own needs. Be adventurous and remove people-pleasing cancer from your mind and behavior. Instead of thinking of how they would feel about you, think of how you want to feel about yourself!

Growing self-confidence includes identifying negative behavior patterns in your ways to rectify them. You can change your life from being a needy codependent to being a badass confident woman, always going after the things that you love. It is your birthright to be happy. Childhood trauma, neglect, or abuse can be healed. Your inner child is awaiting all the love and validation you can give her now, as you reclaim your second Spring and aspire to heal all emotional wounds from the past. Start pouring self-love, wisdom, and self-compassion over them, as they come up for you. Go out and do things for yourself to make YOU happy.

Write down how you really feel about pleasing others versus pleasing yourself, and flip that script completely if you are pleasing others more than necessary to gain their love and approval. There is a marked difference between doing things out of love and doing things TO BE LOVED.

100 | *Self-Confidence Workbook for Women*

Marcee A Martin | 101

The Magic of Making Mistakes

Mistakes are what we make on the path of self-discovery. All great inventors, thinkers, and scientists accept the fact that mistakes take us closer to making new discoveries and finding mystical answers to our questions about life. Similarly, if there is anything at all we can learn from the past as badass confident women, it is to honor our mistakes, to appreciate how our mistakes have strengthened us and groomed us to be our best versions. If we don't learn from our mistakes, how else can we come closer to owning our wisdom? Mistakes bring us closer to perfecting our ideas.

Similarly, every mistake we ever made in our life must be regarded with the same degree of enthusiasm. As hard as it may come across to you, I have realized that mistakes bring us closer to living our best life. Embrace this philosophy and become the best inventor of your life, using your mistakes as a springboard for more growth, greater learning, and new opportunities. As we iron out the creases in the garments of our choice, our appearance and presentation of our best selves also improve. If any of us could go back in a time machine, I am sure there would be many things we would love to change about the past.

I bet though, we would not be shaped by those mistakes anymore, and what a loss that would be too! While we cannot change the past, we can count our blessings NOW and learn to appreciate how all things in our journey have shaped us and how all things now continue to help us expand creatively. The present is here, and the future is still blank! New choices are the gifts of the present and the future. We can only know now what we didn't know in the past when learning and growing from our mistakes. Our level of growth and expansion therefore also depends on our willingness to learn from all mistakes. (Nayar, 2010)

Consider the list of your mistakes: What would you change if you had a time machine? Next to each mistake that you list, determine how it has positively contributed to your life: You may want to think about the person you've become in the process, and how you continue to use those lessons from the past to create new opportunities for yourself now in the present moment. Fill out the entire list!

	Mistake	Positive Contribution
1.		
2.		
3.		
4.		
5.		
6.		
7.		
8.		
9.		
10.		
11.		
12.		
13.		
14.		
15.		
16.		
17.		
18.		
19.		
20.		
21.		
22.		
23.		
24.		

25.		
26.		
27.		
28.		
29.		
30.		
31.		
32.		
33.		
34.		
35.		
36.		
37.		
38.		
39.		
40.		
41.		
42.		
43.		
44.		
45.		
46.		
47.		
48.		
49.		
50.		

Reducing the Overthink

I don't think there is a person on the planet who has not fallen into the trap of overthinking. Unless you're Albert Einstein trying to prove the theory of relativity, overthinking is a negative trap that keeps us stuck in one place for an extended period of time. This is also why it is so important to build healthy relationships with others, keep communication lines open, and be confident enough to trust our intuition in all situations. We must strive to avoid overthinking.

If something is troubling and comes up for you, always aim to find a resolution that feels right. When we aim for resolutions we tie up loose ends. When we tie up loose ends the chances of wasting precious time on unnecessary drama, chaos, and mental stress weaken substantially. When we achieve this, we are then free to be creative, purposeful, and happy beings of love and light.

Badass women who are confident in themselves, are also confident enough to deal with issues head-on, come up with the best resolutions for themselves in all situations, engage in healthy conversations with others, and leave overthinking out of the equation as far as possible. Pour your energy into things that bring you joy, love, and peace. If you are trying to deal with past issues, practice mindfulness in those moments, then let them go.

How Do You Know If You're Overthinking?

Overthinking feels like you have a problem in your life that needs urgent attention, yet you can't seem to go past some inner conflict that a situation has created for you. Overthinking is not the same as self-reflecting. Overthinking can create stress and lead to addictions, mental illness, and short-sighted decision-making. In fact, there might not even be a problem at all, but one that you created from overthinking a situation. Here are some signs of overthinking to help you know you are on this negative frequency:

1. Dwelling too much on past events.

2. Second-guessing your choices.

3. Looking at your perceived mistakes as a burden.

4. Being overly regretful, and remorseful about your past.

5. Imagining worst-case situations.

6. Worrying too much about things that no longer matter.

7. Continuously questioning the motive of others.

8. Becoming suspicious and even paranoid.

There may be times in your life when you do require to come up with resolutions and you may need to go over past events in your mind to reach healthy new resolutions. As long as you aim to let go and reach healthy new resolutions you may need to self-reflect on the issues at hand. It may seem like an overthink. In those situations, do remind yourself of your intention to move on, and come up with a long-term resolution that feels right to you from within. This will keep you from getting stuck in negative emotions relating to a perceived negative situation. (Houstonmethodist, n.d)

The Impact of Overthinking

If you allow overthinking to take over all situations in your life it will have more consequences for you. It will affect how you engage with the world, making you less confident, and more pessimistic to be around. Overthinking will keep you from enjoying life fully at the moment. It will drain your energy and keep you stuck in issues that are beyond your control. Be willing to let things go, especially those things over which you have no control. Exercise care in those things that you can control, and change. Negative thoughts include those that are pessimistic about the future, so cut them out.

We don't tend to overthink positive things in our life. We do tend to overthink when we are being pessimistic and when we become fixated on those things that upset us. This is why overthinking can have a more destructive impact on us, than a constructive one. When we ruminate over stressful incidents we create more anxiety in our life. We also experience more reasons to feel despondent, sad, and hopeless. So avoid overthinking. When you find yourself overthinking, switch it off

106 | *Self-Confidence Workbook for Women*

and get busy with creative, inspiring activities. The past is no more. (Houstonmethodist, n.d)

Here Are More Things That You Can Do When Overthinking Hits You

Do This When Overthinking Hits You	Why It Makes Sense
Don't sweat the small stuff.	You will drive yourself crazy if you don't overlook the small stuff. Let things go quickly and move on.
Follow your instinct but don't jump to conclusions based on it.	Our instinct is animalistic, and often we can sniff out insincerity. However, allow others the space to be themselves without always picturing the worst-case scenario. Rather ask them straight out and communicate your concerns in such situations.
Take a break from the situation.	If you find yourself feeling stressed by overthinking in any situation that is dripping with negativity, take a break and switch it off completely. Come to a decision that will be healthier for you.
Take action on the things that you can control.	Anything that is within your control, act on it, instead of putting up with an upsetting situation. You are worthy of your peace of mind. Reverse a choice if it is bringing you unhappiness.
Let go of the things you cannot control.	Just do it. Let go of the things you cannot control, instead of allowing them to eat you up with negative, persistent, catastrophic thoughts. Simply move on, and cut things out that you cannot control. If your thought patterns are not optimistic but are bringing you down, then it relates to things that are not within your control.

What are some of the things that you find yourself overthinking now? Is it within your control to change it, can you let it go, and come up with resolutions? Or are these things out of your control thus rendering you helpless, and powerless, bringing you down in the confidence department?

Eliminating the Fear From Within

We've all had fears of failure, not being good enough, or being found out for not being good enough. These are all delusions of the mind that have us conditioned to believe in limitations. Eliminating the fear from within is as simple as deciding not to live in fear anymore because you are here: All things in this world must come to an end, but you're worthy of your life, and that is enough in every moment of your existence to do what you love. It is your natural birthright to enjoy life, be happy, and content, and explore your fullest potential. Fear and self-limiting thoughts take root in the subconscious mind.

There are tons of books written on how to eliminate fear, and it all can be traced to past negative experiences, your childhood, being let down, underperforming in the past, and ultimately not believing in yourself. A parent who did not give their child an adequate amount of attention, love, and confidence in their abilities, may have also created that belief in their child's subconscious mind that they will not amount to anything in life. The limitations that our mind accepts over time are all fear-based. They are rooted in negative thoughts, beliefs, and habits which manifest in how we live on a day-to-day basis—unconsciously conditioned to accept limitations.

Marcee A Martin | **109**

Ask Yourself: In what way does fear show up in your life today? Is it a familiar feeling that caused you to give up on many of your dreams in the past?

Here are some simple ways of eliminating your inner fears:

1. Think of all the ways that fear has held you back in the past, and ask yourself what if you decided to go against your fear?

2. Whenever fear appears in your life, pay attention to your thoughts, and turn them around. Ask yourself, "What do I have to lose for not trying? I can only do my best, and see where this takes me!"

3. Expose yourself to your fear. Just go ahead and face your fear head-on. If you're afraid of applying for the dream job because you are afraid of rejection –do it and keep doing it, and keep moving in the direction of your dream regardless of any anticipated rejection.

4. Picture the worst-case scenario and give it everything you got because you're worth it! Do it anyway.

5. When fear shows up tell it: "Welcome back, I see you've shown up in my life again, but guess what, you can sit there, while I shine brilliantly. Watch me and see how you don't have any power over me anymore."

6. Remember that when you try something new or get out of your comfort zone, fear is bound to show up. However, if you believe in your heart that your effort might be worthwhile in the long term, then don't allow fear to hold you back. Your next best adventure awaits you when you decide to release yourself from the clutches of your fears.

7. Practice techniques to calm yourself down when you feel fearful. Slow breathing works for most people, as do meditation techniques aimed at relieving anxiety.

List your fears here and next to each one write down a solution that feels right for you, to lead you further and further away from those fears. Remember: To successfully transform your life, confidence must be your true master and not fear! Your list can be as long as you want it to be. Even a fear that feels silly to write it down, with an aim to transform it. No one is judging you or reading any of your answers.

	My Fear	The Solution
1.	*Example:* Studying a new course in midlife because I was never smart	Pick a short course of interest and sign up.
2.		
3.		
4.		
5.		
6.		
7.		
8.		
9.		
10.		
11.		
12.		
13.		
14.		
15.		
16.		
17.		
18.		
19.		
20.		
21.		
22.		
23.		

24.		
25.		
26.		
27.		
28.		
29.		

Key Takeaways

- Life gets more meaningful at midlife as we aim to unlock our fullest potential.

- The dark side of ourselves all relates to negative traits, thinking patterns, and behaviors that will set us back.

- At 50 you can still rock it without being a people pleaser, and without holding on to fear, indecisiveness, and self-doubt.

- People treat you according to how you teach them to treat you.

- We all make mistakes, but learning from mistakes is key to achieving long-term growth.

- Midlife is about self-reflection, to heal the shadow parts of ourselves.

- The distorted, negative perceptions have kept us away from really exploring our full potential.

- Let your cup be filled with inspiration daily, instead of unrealistic expectations of yourself.

- We must get rid of those incorrect, often distorted labels that we've attached to some of our life experiences.

- Whenever a negative thought about yourself emerges, flip that switch immediately from being negative to positive.

- Make being positive a healthy new habit!

- Practicing mindfulness more often will help you cope with challenging situations.

- Avoid overthinking it will create psychological distress more than offer solutions.

In the next chapter, we will learn how two one percenter grew their fortunes and committed to a life of purpose and vision.

CHAPTER 5

HOW THE TOP 1% THINKS

People do not decide to become extraordinary. They decide to accomplish great things according to what is truly meaningful to them. –Marcee A Martin

Work is Love Made Visible

There are no shortcuts to success. Only the long road. The path includes dedication, resilience, imagination, and determination to get to the destination of success, wealth and even immortality in some cases. We all have our heroes' or "sheroes." A woman who I greatly admire who made it amongst the one-percenters is J.K. Rowling. She is a person of great strength and character. I admire her for her resilience and the amazing courage and confidence she has displayed throughout her life. It paid off greatly for her when it mattered the most. After learning more about her journey, like so many others, one can only marvel at her achievements.

Work is love made visible, and living with a sense of purpose can lead to marvelous new adventures, regrowth, and soulful validation. A lot of women today, do get their sense of purpose from the work they do, as J.K. Rowling does. Her past was filled with sadness, interspersed with moments of happiness, and some success before she hit rock bottom. It was during this time that she kept at her writing and experienced a sense of liberation, despite the depression she also suffered from at the time. The one thing she did regardless of what she was going through during those hard, poverty-stricken days was write her book, *Harry Potter and the Philosopher's Stone*. Now at midlife, J.K. is a whopping success, and life couldn't be rosier.

She is enjoying financial independence today but not because that was her goal. She was barely able to pay her rent when she was writing her book. However, achieving financial success was a big deal, to a struggling author, single mum, and survivor of domestic violence. She suffered deep losses at the cusp of her writing career, in her thirties. Stunningly that one book which she did not give up on, made her a one percenter in the world, along with the follow-up books in her *Harry Potter* series. Rowling was driven to succeed by an inner vision that called to her. Not giving up on it is what gave her purpose. She chose to answer the call of inspiration without knowing that fortune and fame were awaiting her.

I suppose that is one of the biggest lessons to learn from Rowling's rise to fame: She was able to captivate the imagination of the world using her own. Had she doubted her ability to do so or her inner vision, greatness would not have manifested for her in this lifetime. It was destiny that called out to her. At the time when she started writing her first fantasy book, she was broke. Many people in her shoes might've given up and missed out on a chance of greatness. Not J.K. Rowling. She kept writing even when she couldn't afford to pay the rent. Stunningly, her destiny changed when she became the first author in the world to reach the one-billion-dollar mark when that one book took the world by storm!

The Great Secret to Success and Being a One-Percenter

The one percenters are those who own 43.7% of the world's wealth (Cayalag, 2021). A lot of people have asked them what it means to have amassed a fortune for themselves. For J.K. Rowling, a woman who made it in her thirties as an author, it was about "not giving up" on her Harry Potter dream. She had many reasons to give up. The odds were stacked up against her, as it was for most other one percenters. However, publishing her book was the only option she gave herself. The rest is history, as the saying goes. There is no great secret to uncover when it comes to achieving success at a global level. It really comes down to believing in something greater than yourself and going after it with passion, dedication, and unflinching faith in your ability to achieve it.

Wealth is how the Universe rewards you for the mission you give yourself. In case, her work touched the hearts of billions of people across the planet and she was paid accordingly. The Universe applauds those who take physical action on their dream. That isn't a secret. It is plain to see today. There have been many great women in history who have defied the odds stacked against them to follow a dream, an inner calling as they call it. (Cayalag, 2021)

The Genius and Luck Combination Work Like a Charm

Another British female author who lived two centuries before J.K. Rowling didn't earn much money for her books, and she did them in secret under a pen name at the time, "written by a lady." Her name was Jane Austin. She wanted to be a writer in the 18th- century when women were frowned upon for taking up any kind of profession, including writing. Today she is celebrated as one of the greatest women writers of all time.

Her picture also made it on the 10-pound note in Britain. Movies were made of her books too. However, Jane Austin died in poverty and she mainly lived her life one step away from being destitute. Wealth and fame remained elusive for 18th-century Austin. She died penniless at the age of 41. Still, she did get her happy ending. Her name lives on in the hearts and minds of those who appreciate her stories, even today. There is no value sufficient enough to ascribe to women who have defied all odds to achieve great success.

Marcee A Martin | **117**

If Jane Austin was allowed to be a professional writer in her time without controversy attached to it, she too would be among the one percenters without any doubt. The work put in with dedication becomes a priceless contribution to the world, and that is something that all one-percenters enjoy. A stroke of genius, expressed with confidence and passion, and a stroke of luck changed their destinies as it can yours too if you believe in your purpose and inner vision. It is never too late to decide to take up a vision larger than yourself for the love of it.

Follow Your Heart and Act Without Hesitation

The vision for both Dr. John Demartini and J.K. Rowling was to follow their passion. It was of course much bigger than they both had anticipated. They were simply following their hearts. The journey was also the destination for them both, which is why they did not hesitate when those inner nudges of inspiration called out to them. The act of writing and unleashing their imagination, putting words to paper is what compelled them both. In that sense, the vision was larger than who they were. They were therefore able to transcend the limitations of the challenging circumstances they both faced in unique ways during their individual lifetimes.

Rowling's train from Manchester to London was delayed by four hours on a day in the mid-'90s when inspiration struck. During that time, the characters of Harry Potter, Ron Weasley, and Hermoine Granger popped up in her mind. She explored their characters in her imagination throughout the train trip to London and without hesitation or second-guessing herself she produced an entire series for Harry Potter fans. Both the books and the movies produced amassed her a fortune, and they will continue to outlive her. Before writing the Harry Potter series, Rowling wrote adult novels, nothing remotely close to the characters or adventures she conjured up in her Harry Potter series. Inspiration strikes when you least expect it to. Not giving up on yourself remains a key factor to keep possibilities flowing in your life.

118 | *Self-Confidence Workbook for Women*

What are some of the compelling moments of inspiration that occurred in your life? The Universe is an abundant place, even if you may have missed exploring some of your earlier moments of inspirational ideas, there will always be more waiting to be explored. Meditation, and practicing self-care reduces stress and in turn, will also stimulate your imagination. Feeling good about yourself opens up a natural confidence, and will spur more creativity in your life. It will help you to tap more into your inner life to explore new inspirational ideas in midlife. Never give up on yourself.

Write them down here now to recapture them. Then open your heart to exploring new ideas all the time, as a constant flow of never ending possibilities!

Follow Your Inspiration

The point is to follow it, just as J.K. Rowling did when she first glimpsed the Harry Potter characters in her imagination. When the voice of the vision is louder than all the opinions and things going on in your life, you have begun the journey of self-mastery. Be, do, and have all that you need. It will manifest regardless of the trials and tribulations if you believe in the vision and commit to bringing it to life.

Every challenge is an opportunity for growth, expansion, and confidence. If you embrace a larger more compelling vision it will take hold and uplift you to experience new heights of success. Confidence is not just about having the perfect conditions in your life to support it; it is what will help you to transcend the imperfect conditions that will perpetually show up in your life to challenge you! You don't need to be rich, or super affluent to follow those initial inner callings of inspiration. You don't even need to be acknowledged, as in the case of Jane Austin. You just need to believe in it, if it feels right for you!

Jane Austin believed in her writing, and her father did support her in her writing, by encouraging it with his approval. That was all that mattered to Jane. The fact that women were not properly acknowledged as important contributors to the literary world did not faze her. She would

120 | *Self-Confidence Workbook for Women*

stare out at the countryside from the window where she sat in her home at Hampshire cottage, allowing her imagination to take her away to dreams of love, and happiness. She wrote six novels at Hampshire Cottage, which is a museum today in her honor.

J.K. Rowling was living in a rat-infested flat when she was writing the first book of her Harry Potter series in the mid-'90s. Broken psychologically from a divorce, and facing a deep depression, the inner vision continued to inspire her. She became relentless and desired to complete the book: Harry Potter and the Philosopher's Stone, even after suffering from depression. Even through all of that, and taking up a teaching course to earn a living, Rowling kept on with her writing.

She was earning a mere 22 pounds per week doing secretarial work and she was also dependent on a government allowance. After her book was published and her popularity grew, she bought a new home for herself from the royalties she received. She ended up selling millions of copies of all her books in the Harry Potter series, all across the globe. In 1999, Warner Brothers purchased the film rights for the first two Harry Potter movies for one million dollars. It was only the start of more money, movies, and stories to share with the world for J.K. Rowling.

Your Desire to Succeed Must Be Stronger Than All External Factors

Being driven by a strong desire to accomplish a vision that comes from within is key to accomplishing a unique success in the world. If you believe in abundance, and if you are confident enough to hold that vision up high in front of you, there is no telling what great success awaits you. Rowling was broke, unable to pay her rent, divorced, lonely, and a survivor of domestic violence. However, her first Harry Potter book took shape during those dark days.

She captivated the world's imagination when it was finally published after being constantly rejected by publishers before she got her lucky break. She couldn't even afford to make copies of the first manuscript. Being relentless in the pursuit of her objective, she typed out a few more copies on her typewriter and sent them off to publishers. Your desire to succeed must therefore trump the external factors that appear to work against you.

Life is about perception more than it is about what is going on outside of you. Another one percenter is Dr. John Demartini. He is a world-renowned human behavior specialist who travels the world throughout the year to spread his research and teachings in human development, and to encourage others to build a life that is authentically aligned with their inner vision. He was once an illiterate high school dropout who was told that he wouldn't amount to anything in life. His desire to succeed trumped all of that when he discovered his inner calling.

Use the Power of Authenticity to Change Your Life

When John Demartini met Paul Bragg, the pioneer of health food stores in the United States in 1976 in Hawaii, Demartini was homeless and living in a tent. He was also illiterate. He was determined to succeed as a surfboard maker. However, when he attended a yoga class with Bragg leading the way, he discovered a new vision for his life. This new vision earned him the right to be among the one-percenters in the world today. Before meeting Bragg, Demartini believed what everyone else told him, that he wouldn't amount to anything in life, which is why he settled for surfing and making surfboards.

Demartini didn't know any better. However, that one night in Hawaii, that one man with one message changed his life and led him to a new path of education, and studying human behavior. He is today regarded as a polymath and a genius. It was Paul Bragg who also gave John Demartini the affirmation that night to repeat every day to himself, "I am a genius, and I apply my wisdom." (Huffpost, n.d.) The power of authenticity is what we are all striving to achieve as we heal and expand our awareness. Dr. Demartini and J.K. Rowling, like so many others, decided to follow an inner vision that surpassed the outer realities of their lives.

At the time, it seemed like a big task to achieve. However, persistence, and a commitment to a larger vision, eventually resulted in its manifestation. They did not set out to become amongst the one percenters in the world. Their vision was authentic and it is that authenticity, that people bought into. It nourished billions of people around the globe, inspired new thoughts, and created a ripple effect for everyone concerned. Authenticity is the soul's desire to expand to reach and achieve a great sense of purpose and accomplishment. Getting to a place of authenticity, which is free from the layers of socialized acceptable standards includes trusting ourselves, and our inner vision. We must have a natural confidence to explore sources of inspiration.

Think about this: What may have held you back in the past from fully exploring your talents and inspiring larger-than-life ideas? For example, as in Dr. Demartini's case, people told him repeatedly that he won't amount to anything in life. He believed them until someone else told him something new; that he can be a genius if that's what he wanted. An awareness of what may have held you back in the past is the first step to begin transcending those limitations. Explore it here below.

The Push of a Little Confidence Will Reshape Your Destiny

Yes, a good dose of confidence is needed. In J.K. Rowling's case it was her confidence in her characters, her imagination, and having nothing to lose that gave her the courage to pursue her writing. Of course, she always wanted to be a great writer. It was her childhood dream. In Dr. Demartini's case he never heard anyone tell him before that he could be a genius and amount to something more than what he was, an illiterate high school dropout. Hearing someone believe in him, gave him confidence, and hope. The dream in both cases was not to be a billionaire. The dream of success was to achieve something rewarding and inspiring from within. That is the value of following a vision from within. It becomes the life purpose that defines the destiny you are bound to fulfill when you commit to that inner vision.

Confidence, therefore, is the elixir to achieving greatness. Even if it's just a little dose at a time that is taking you forward, the magic still works. All you require is a little dose of self-belief, and self-confidence each day in your vision to keep you moving forward one step at a time. Despite the depths of despair, depression, and suicidal thoughts, Rowling experienced along the way of her journey to success, she still returned to her writing. She also sought professional help from a therapist during her depression and just kept writing, even doubling up on her efforts when she decided to sign up for a teaching course.

Confidence is also that small voice in the darkness that says "It's okay we will try again tomorrow. It's another day to keep doing what we love doing." Every page written was part of what made the Harry Potter series a whopping success. So keep working on each page of the story of your life. You're starting a new chapter in midlife. Focus on reshaping this journey one page at a time according to a new inner vision that will undoubtedly emerge during this important transition in your life. You will get to your destination if you are determined and committed enough to manifest your life purpose and vision. That is confidence!

What are some of the misconceptions you've held in the past about confidence? Did you think that confident people had to be perfect, look a certain way, or be smarter than others? Maybe you think only the rich are allowed to be confident? Start to recognize confidence as that little ray of hope that emerges just to push you on a little further each day, even when you're feeling more depressed than happy! It is a state of being congruent with all that is important to you and has very little to do with what you have or don't have at any given point in time. You will see everything as being on the way out as opposed to being in the way when you believe in its magic. Write down your misconceptions or false beliefs about confidence below. Read them over, and begin to see confidence as a powerful small voice at times that whispers to you words of hope and encouragement.

126 | *Self-Confidence Workbook for Women*

Don't Wait for the Perfect Conditions for Success To Arrive

As you've discovered from Dr. Demartini's and J.K. Rowling's stories, there is no such thing as success coming to you because you have the perfect conditions in place for it to arrive on time. Those are the excuses some of us make to delay our chances of achieving the success we deserve. There have been many entrepreneurs who have delayed their success by a few years as they waited for their living conditions to improve. You can survive and thrive at the same time if you are willing to get down to the work now, to manifest the vision and purpose of your life regardless of what you have or don't have at your disposal.

Make do with the skills that are available to you and the things you can do now to start building on the dream. Rowling had an imagination, and a typewriter, even though she was living in poverty, and dealing with so many painful personal issues. Friends gave her some money along the way to help her keep a roof over her head. She found some work on the side to keep an income coming in and took up teaching English as another way of earning an income while she was writing her bestseller Harry Potter and the Philosopher's Stone, the first book in the Harry Potter series.

Writing her book remained important to Rowling, even in the midst of a breakdown. She followed her intuition and worked hard to get her book published. Her work on the Harry Potter series has immortalized her as an author. All she ever wanted to do when she was young was to write books. You must pursue what you love regardless of the chaos in your life. Make no excuses. Be on fire, and be determined.

How do some of the external factors in your life challenge you at present? Ask yourself: How can you start pursuing your inner vision today with what is available to you now, without using external circumstances as an excuse for getting in the way of following your dreams?

128 | *Self-Confidence Workbook for Women*

Living Life With Purpose

Life purpose does matter as in the case of Dr. Demartini and J.K. Rowling. Dr. Demartini found his true life purpose after attending a yoga class. Before that, he thought he was always going to be a surfer. Not that surfing is not a great sport, but it was much smaller than Dr. Demartini's true life purpose, which emerged during the meditative state he entered in the yoga session. It was an inner vision that called him to his true life purpose, as was the case with Rowling. A life purpose is something magical that you can connect with when you reach deep within yourself.

It is always there, and YES, it does depend on recognizing it when it emerges in your life, through visions, inspiration, ideas, and creativity. If you look at your life upon closer inspection you are bound to see patterns emerge that are linked to a life purpose. Perhaps you always had one, and were drawn towards achieving something more meaningful but lacked the courage or confidence to pursue it further.

Take some time out to think about how your life purpose is emerging in your life now. You may not have all the answers, but they are bound to be signed. What do you think is your life purpose now in midlife? How is your life purpose showing up in your life? Think about the activities that are most meaningful to you. It might reflect a new calling or an ongoing inspirational idea that keeps emerging.

130 | *Self-Confidence Workbook for Women*

The Natural Abundance Mindset

Having an abundant mindset is about believing and accepting that you are always deserving of more, which is always on the way to you. When something appears not to be working in your favor, it is an abundant mindset that will release you from moments of frustration and resistance. Anyone with an abundant mindset will allow failure to take place in some instances. They will see it as an abundant sign from the Universe that something better is on the way! Embracing natural abundance will help you to excitedly bounce back quickly after suffering a loss. You will naturally align yourself with the vast expansive field of the Universe of possibility. It is important to start feeling more abundant regardless of your material possession. Below are the signs of an abundant mindset (Chopra, 2019).

1. Feelings of unlimited possibilities are always emerging.
2. You feel happier, fulfilled, and satisfied with life.
3. You embrace both support and challenge with equal enthusiasm.
4. You do give and receive support and items more easily to others, knowing that more is always on the way to you!
5. You feel expansive, creative, and unlimited in potential.
6. You manifest abundance in your life more naturally.
7. You experience greater innovation and produce exceptional results in all areas of your life.
8. You feel more confident in yourself to go after what you want.
9. You are secure within yourself and learn from the past productively.
10. You naturally embrace every aspect of your life and avoid using negative labels to judge your actions.
11. You do love and support yourself and you know and appreciate the value of your own time.
12. You use setbacks as opportunities to create comebacks in your life.
13. You support your ongoing growth and development.

How abundant do you feel right now in your life? Do you think there is room for improvement, and how can you change from feeling less abundant to embracing a naturally abundant mentality if you look at your life right now and some of the issues that you are facing?

The Power of Shifting Perspective

It is possible to shift your mindset to embrace a more abundant one. If you completed the previous exercise you may have identified how you can start creating new outcomes in your life when you decide to shift your perspective from accepting limitations to embracing abundant new possibilities, opportunities, and outcomes. When we are choosing to be more positive we will naturally start feeling better about our prospects. We will also be able to see many new solutions on the horizon. We are keen to understand events better and embrace all new experiences as meaningful encounters.

We often tend to catastrophize things in our life when we are filled with negativity, and we tend to optimize on opportunities when we feel more abundant. Developing a solidly abundant frame of reference will keep you growing on a positive trajectory in life, and it will help you to experience more blessings, miracles, and expanded consciousness. Here's how you can create an abundant mindset for yourself:

1. **Practice mindfulness.** As we have already explored in Chapter 3, practicing mindfulness more often will help you to become an objective observer as opposed to letting your thoughts control you.

2. **Journaling.** This will help you to monitor your emotions, perspective, and events, to continuously assess the cause of action needed to stay inspired, strong, and resilient throughout your journey.

3. **Count your blessings by practicing gratitude.** Count your blessings whenever you start feeling more limited than abundant. Remind yourself how far you've journeyed in life, and be thankful for everything.

4. **Monitor your thoughts to reframe them when they are negative.** In other words, consciously make an effort to support yourself as opposed to sabotaging yourself with negative thoughts, and feelings. Be more realistic, and optimistic about everything.

Marcee A Martin | **133**

5. **Identify your strengths.** In moments of weakness or feelings of inadequacy, identify your strengths and keep moving in that direction optimistically. Remember that we are all unique, and you have yours to be proud of.

6. **Question your motives.** Keep questioning yourself, your motives, aspirations, attitudes, and beliefs to continuously expand to feel more abundant.

7. **Avoid thinking along the lines of should've and would've.** Avoid living in regret about any of your past choices. Focus instead on the can-do's in your life, and keep moving forward. Honor your past, present and future choices without judgment while being open to learning from all of life's generous lessons.

8. **Focus on making progress.** There will always be setbacks and challenges that will come up for us. This is why it is important to do what you love. The self-motivation to keep moving forward will see all things as learning curves. Perfection is unrealistic so don't count on it. Rather work on producing excellent results that are meaningful to you.

9. **Look at your environment and the company you keep.** You are on average the company of the five people you regularly interact with. Look at the quality of your associations with others as well as your environment and ask yourself how they are serving you for your optimal growth. If not, make some changes to avoid the limited perceptions of others influencing your mind negatively.

10. **Keep an open mind.** If you are serious about succeeding then it is important to continuously assess the value of your goals and ideas, stick to the plan or make some tweaks to allow for new fresh ideas and perspectives to emerge and reshape your life. (Kukteliones, n.d).

Task: Take one limited thought, or a few that are constantly showing up for you, and examine how you can reshape this thought in a way that will support a powerful shift in your perspective.

134 | *Self-Confidence Workbook for Women*

Marcee A Martin | 135

Key Takeaways

- There are no shortcuts to success.

- The path to success includes dedication, resilience, imagination, and determination

- Work is love made visible, and living with a sense of purpose can lead to marvelous new adventures.

- Wealth is how the Universe rewards you for the mission you give yourself.

- It is never too late to decide to take up a vision larger than yourself for the love of it.

- Don't wait for the perfect conditions for success to arrive. Start now!

- The power of authenticity is what we are all striving to achieve as we heal and expand in awareness.

- It is possible to shift your mindset to embrace a more abundant one.

- Having an abundant mindset is about believing and accepting that you are always deserving of more than what is always on the way to you.

- Your desire to succeed must be greater than all external factors that appear to be on your way.

- Life is about perception more than it is about what is going on outside of you.

- How we deal with our challenges is also based on our mindset and perception.

136 | *Self-Confidence Workbook for Women*

CHAPTER 6

GETTING THE FUEL

Every little path that you follow to rediscover yourself, holds the opportunity for greatness! –Marcee A Martin

The Driving Force

It is not that difficult to discover your driving force in midlife. The driving force is what will move you into action positively, to take your life to a whole new level of self-exploration. Driving force is an energy that comes from within when you are motivated, inspired, and enthused by the prospect of achieving something meaningful to you. Anne Driscoll, as you discovered in Chapter 1, found her driving force at the age of 62. It was always there, lying dormant but covered up by the layers of self-doubt and questions about surviving, thriving, and earning well in a new country.

Moving to Ireland was a dream she cherished in her heart for many years before being able to make that happen. When a new solution presented itself to her, her driving force or motivation returned and she was on purpose again, on fire, and working smartly to get accepted into a scholarship program which also landed her a job when she was successful with her five-page business proposal.

Sometimes it can be one statement or one interesting article that you come across as you surf the net, that can change the direction of your life. Or as in Driscoll's case, it could be something that someone said to you, that offered you a glimpse into a new possibility. So, if you are not feeling a driving force at present it's okay, it will happen as long as there is a desire to discover a driving force in your life to give it more meaning, purpose, and color!

No doubt, as in my case and that of so many other women, getting unstuck from our comfort zones is perhaps one of the biggest challenges we face in midlife. We've spent half a century—if you want to measure our time on earth based on years—doing things in a certain way, living according to a set of beliefs, whether they were limiting or not, and presenting ourselves in the world in a manner that resonated with those beliefs. When we reach midlife our beliefs are changing especially as we begin to question the past, aimed at uncovering what we may have missed. It is a natural process of aspiring to bring back meaning, purpose, and fun.

Getting Unstuck From Your Comfort Zone

The midlife transition is stressful when we realize that we crave change, yet we are unable to determine how that change should manifest. Well, I am here to tell you that it doesn't have to happen all at once. Think of discovering yourself again at midlife as an entirely new journey unfolding before you one day at a time. Even if the change you are implementing now is focused on creating a new inspiring self-care routine for yourself, that's super. Go for it with full gusto. Every time we start doing something new or implement new changes in our life, we are creating new possibilities to experience more creativity. That is exactly what you need as a foundation to keep moving towards finding something that will ultimately lead you to your biggest "self-discovery moment," when you uncover the driving force.

You may ask, what is your comfort zone? Everyone's comfort zone is different. However, it is often the zone you enter when things are

138 | *Self-Confidence Workbook for Women*

going reasonably well, you are in a fixed routine, and you are earning reasonably well, but something is missing, yet you cannot quite place your finger on it! When you enter the comfort zone, it's like you've entered a plateau area. Everything is just flat. There is no climbing, or new learning taking place, nor is there clarity on what you could do next to get rid of the flatness you feel inside of you.

The comfort zone feels like this: You've done some pretty interesting things in your life, yet there are some things you haven't fully explored in your life, and you're too comfortable to admit it or decide on a new path of growth, experimentation, learning, and creativity. There are ways though that you can explore to start getting out of that comfort zone, gradually. It doesn't have to include taking a very big leap of faith into the unknown. You can start experimenting with new growth experiences in small steps. All steps do add up, so you are bound to discover something new in that process of self-discovery.

If you always wanted to spend more time cooking, for example, but neglected that in the past, then put that on your midlife bucket list and give it a shot. Work through your bucket list one item at a time. Who knows where it could lead you? Or if it was painting that you neglected in the past or playing the piano more, then commit to making time to explore those talents. You might strike a note that resonates with an inner driving force somewhere in these midlife episodes of rediscovering yourself.

Explore your comfort zone: Think about your life, and ask yourself, if you are at a plateau right now. What does it feel like to you, and do you have any ideas to explore to get yourself out of your comfort zone?

140 | *Self-Confidence Workbook for Women*

Finding Your Purpose

Finding your core, or taking the journey to discover your core in midlife, is the same as deciding to fully come alive! Getting out of your comfort zone is bound to add lots of color, and creativity. Going from black and white to full color is exactly what every midlife woman needs to get unstuck from all the negativity of the past. Bring out the paintbrush and blank canvas, to start painting a life of new possibility. If you are feeling that flatness inside of you, then that is a sign that you need to liven things up. Why settle for mediocrity just because you're a midlifer?

You are not alone if you wake up in the morning feeling restless, dissatisfied, and not purposeful anymore. Your life may have been interesting when you were younger working your way to the top of your game or learning new things that gave you purpose. Most midlife women feel flat in the mornings when they haven't fully discovered the new direction to take in their lives. You can find a new purpose. Learning doesn't have to stop just because we are older than we once were. Finding a new purpose or redefining an old one is a powerful way of reclaiming meaning and fulfillment. Here are some steps to guide you to your life purpose.

1. **Reflect on your values and passions.** Think about what your new values are now at midlife, and how they have changed over the years. Change is a sign of growth. Embrace that change and link your values to possible new interests, which can end up becoming a new passion.

2. **Experiment with new activities.** Go ahead and take the step, try out new things, and stop procrastinating by working through your bucket list. There might be some things on that list that can spur on a new passion and purpose that will redefine the next chapters of your life.

3. **Seek support from others.** Join a midlife social club and start connecting with other women going through the same comfort zone slump as you are. You might pick up some good ideas from them and be supported by them. You could also hire a life coach

to help you identify new things of interest for experimentation. You might end up carving a whole new career for yourself in a new direction. The possibilities are endless.

4. **Embrace uncertainty.** Embrace new days doing new things, and not knowing with absolute certainty where the journey will take you, except for the experience of adding more color to your life and welcoming in new possibilities. Be open to new experiences, make some new friends, and try on some new clothes and new hairstyles. Be explorative, and fun. It will bring out your creative side and might lead you down interesting rabbit holes of self-discovery.

5. **Cook up a storm.** If cooking is your thing, then you can learn some pointers from Julia Child who took up cooking and blogging at the age of 49. She became quite a sensation. Invite friends and family over for dinner, and impress them with your new hobby. Make a video, and write some blogs, see where that will take you! If you are feeling charitable and want to connect to a worthy cause, raise some money from your cooking, and feel great about your contribution.

6. **Audition for a talent show.** You might just end up being the next singing sensation like Susan Boyle became when she auditioned for Britain's Got Talent at the age of 47. She was an absolute miracle and made a new singing career for herself. Many people were in tears when they heard her voice and witnessed new talent that was so unbelievably extraordinary.

So you see, there are limitless possibilities to explore, even in midlife. You will experience increased motivation, energy, and zest for life once you start reigniting that driving force behind a new passionate interest. This is exactly what we all need to do to wake up every morning feeling like the sun is just bursting out of the sky again. We cannot reclaim our younger days by being regretful, so it's pointless doing that. Rather settle for more now, and better. We can reclaim our sense of purpose and aliveness by exploring new interests and pulling out the stops to become our full passionate selves in midlife.

142 | *Self-Confidence Workbook for Women*

There is no such thing as becoming trapped in our need for constant success, and growth. The human spirit is always on a quest to conquer, achieve, and explore. This is how we've gotten to the information age today. It is embedded in us to live inspiring purposeful lives. The only limitations are the ones that we decide on. As long as your intrinsic desire is to succeed, to feel fulfilled, and to expand your horizons, fulfillment will come to you at any age.

There are no rules that say when it is enough to have enough of life. Nor do we need to apologize as women to be all that we can when we reach midlife. We owe it to ourselves to enjoy our second Spring and to ensure that when we reach the next decade we are not sitting with more regrets and issues to work past. Taking care of our physical and psychological health remains key to enjoying the best years of our lives: That journey includes being passionate, purposeful, and powerful! (Voll, 2023)

Worksheet for Developing Your Driving Force

Follow these steps regularly to get back in touch with your natural driving force!

Action to Take	Why It Is Important
Set goals	Achieve clarity on what you want to achieve. Setting goals stimulates the prefrontal cortex of your brain into action. This is important as you now have a roadmap to reignite purpose in your life.
Stick to them	Stick to your goals, and chunk them down into bite-sized tasks to achieve daily. If you are planning to write a book, then you can make writing 1000 words per day a bite-sized daily goal.

Create a timeline	Ensure that you know and understand just how long it is going to take you to fulfill your goals. It will once again give you the motivation to keep moving toward the goals you've set for yourself.
Commit to learning something new	Identify new things that you can learn to enhance your journey and the achievement of your goals.
Assess your progress regularly	Regularly assess your progress to determine just how much you've grown, and how far you've come in your life.
Create a support system	Reach out to coaches, mentors, or other professionals in your field of interest and join a learning group or a support group to keep your energy levels high, focused, and enthused about your new mission.
Reward Yourself	Reward yourself along the way for taking an inspiring new journey!
Celebrate the milestones	For every milestone that you've achieved in your life, celebrate it and applaud yourself accordingly. For example, you could also post a pic of every milestone that you've reached and post it on social media. It will be a great encouragement for others who are searching for a new purpose.
Keep moving forward	Just keep moving forward all the time without second guessing yourself. Remind yourself that failure is not an option and that your days of playing small and accepting limitations are long over.

Stick to your self-care	Midlife is your second spring break! You deserve to look and feel great from the inside out. So stick to your self-care, and do not neglect yourself.
Keep exploring new opportunities	Once you get going with learning new things, and exploring new creative outlets, you can expect new opportunities to start opening up for you, so keep moving forward, and explore those new opportunities. Add them as new goals, and create a new timeline.

Key Takeaways

- Driving force is an energy that comes from within. In midlife, it is important to get in touch with that energy!

- Getting unstuck from our comfort zones is perhaps one of the biggest challenges we face in midlife.

- Make getting unstuck a priority especially if you are seeking new growth.

- Everyone's comfort zone looks different. Explore yours to start expanding again in new directions.

- Finding your inner drive doesn't have to include taking a big leap of faith into the unknown.

- Every step you take in new directions to rediscover yourself will lead to interesting results for you in your life.

- You can find a new purpose in midlife. Learning doesn't have to stop just because we are older.

- We are here to learn as long as we are alive and enthused to have more fun, contribute, and feel purposeful.

- Splash some color in your life, and make a list of new interests and passions that you wish to explore.

Marcee A Martin | **145**

- Remember that change is the only constant in life. If you want to fly again then embrace change.
- Feeling flat is what it is like when you are stuck in a comfort zone.
- Try out new things and stop procrastinating.
- It's time to spread your wings and be your fully capable, beautiful, and powerful self.
- There is no such thing as not being enough, having enough, or doing enough. When your cup is overflowing with love, you are always enough!

CHAPTER 7

WORKING ON THE FOUNDATION OF SELF-CONFIDENCE

There is no greater gift that you can give yourself than the confidence to fully embrace all that you are with a purposeful, and inspiring mission. –Marcee A Martin

Control What You Think About Yourself

When we started this journey together I told you that I discovered the secret to changing my life. That lies in the power of creating new thoughts, and completely flipping the script, which is what I was aiming for when I made up my mind to move out from the darkness of negativity and into the light of my soul. This is where I believe our true creative genius lies. It is the mind that must be trained properly in such a way that we can rewrite our destinies. It is the mind that blocks out that inspiring light of genius and creativity when become consumed with negativity. Everything that we need is inside of us, and not outside of us.

We must therefore tap into our inner world of thoughts, feelings, and choices to exert power in our outer world. What we think about is what we will manifest and bring about. Also, how we feel about all situations including ourselves is always based on the quality of the thoughts we entertain daily. Just remember that in every moment of sadness, and darkness a new dawn awaits you. Our minds are very creative. All you need to do is have one positive thought that will outshine the negative ones. If that one positive thought is, "Today no matter what happens I am committed to being happy," then brilliant, you've set your intention and your subconscious mind will take over and remind you of this commitment when things get tough.

If you commit to being happier then you can consciously push out the stress factors that crop up in the day. If you find that your work is feeling tiresome, and you are lacking in energy and spirit to go on, simply flip that switch again from negative to positive. Remind yourself how wonderful it will feel to earn that much-needed vacation, and how amazing it is to be doing what you love with people who appreciate your contribution. Also, be practical to attend to your physical needs later by getting proper nutrition and rest.

Flipping the internal switch from negative to positive retrains your subconscious mind to stay on its cause, instead of self-sabotaging your efforts and derailing you from your commitment to reach certain goals. You have to make a conscious effort to train your subconscious mind in such a way that it supports you and does not work against you. Negative thoughts that are allowed to flourish in your subconscious mind will end up being counterproductive and will create mental obstacles. If you say to yourself often, "I'm always feeling so tired these days. Why does life always have to be so difficult for me?" you will begin to believe the negativity.

Our Thoughts Are Vibrations That Become Our Reality

Life will get more difficult for you when you believe that it's always going to be this way. We may not even be consciously aware of how our thoughts can pull us down. That is exactly what happens when we believe more in our negative thoughts.

Our thoughts and beliefs are commands that we give to our subconscious mind. When we accept limiting beliefs about ourselves and our potential, it will manifest exactly in accordance with those beliefs. If you hear a song on the radio for example, and your mind starts wandering to a memory from the past that is not very pleasant, associated with that song, your entire mood can shift from feeling optimistic to feeling depressed, agitated, and moody.

Everything we think about and feel we bring about. In the same way, the past comes to life when we overthink it, and brood over it more than is necessary. This, in turn, can negatively impact your level of productivity and it could further impact other habits that you've adopted to numb the negative feelings and emotions. For example, if you tend to eat more to compensate for a perceived lack of love and support in your life, then you will continue to use this habit to make you feel better. If the song reminded you of a past heartbreak you might find yourself turning to food after you started brooding over the past when you heard the song on the radio.

As a result, you may not be able to enjoy your evening meditation at all because of those earlier toxic thoughts or even get a good night's rest. Recognize those triggers that bring back unpleasant memories from the past and flip the inner dialogue from negative to positive. Turn the dial on the radio and listen to something else. Our thoughts have power over us, and it is time that you decide to take that power back!

Use powerful affirmations daily: Write down self-affirmations to replace your usual negative thoughts about yourself, and also work on changing those thoughts that come up for you when you experience higher levels of stress. We can have on average 6,000 thoughts a day, and if you are anything like I was in the past, most of them were more negative thoughts than positive thoughts about ourselves! Let's get through this list completely and fill up the page. Start turning that inner dial on your radio to a frequency that matches positive thoughts and feelings.

Negative Thought	Powerful Affirmation
For example, "I'm just hopeless. I never seem to be able to complete projects!"	I am more than capable of completing them successfully, and I intend on completing all of my projects successfully.
For example, "I hate this job! Everyone else is smarter than me."	I chose this job because I am very skilled and talented and valued for this greatly.

150 | *Self-Confidence Workbook for Women*

Marcee A Martin | 151

Determining the Values

When we reach midlife we have powerful new realizations, and this, in turn, shifts the goalpost for us in so many ways. Unless we are consciously in tune with the changes taking place within, we will not be consciously aware of the shift taking place around our values. This inner shift of values is part of the intense transition we experience in midlife. Our values naturally shift as do our beliefs, based on the lessons we've learned and our growing experience. We outgrow our youth, as we enter the second Spring of our lives. It is time in midlife to expand our growth, and nature calls us to explore a new identity. Like a butterfly, we must shed the cocoon to spread our wings in the second Spring of our life.

While dating might have been a priority in our younger years to find the most suitable partner, in midlife companionship and friendship might replace that need, especially if you've had your fair share of complicated relationships. Likewise, new interests will replace old ones, and we may want to for example completely change the area where we live to accommodate a new lifestyle or preference. Maybe city life worked great for us when we climbed the corporate ladder, but starting a new business in a suburban area may have more appeal now. It is perfectly natural to rethink your priorities at midlife and to desire or carve a chance to reignite your passion for life.

Determining what your new values are as you transition to your midlife years, is an important stepping stone to realizing your new purpose, and the new destiny you aim to fulfill for the remaining years of your life. Holding on to old values while undergoing intense changes will create more inner friction than you realize. There will be a disconnect taking place emotionally between who you are becoming and the journey you've already traveled. So achieving profound clarity on your shifting values will give you a strong sense of purpose and direction.

It is time to let go of some of our old dreams as we may have outgrown them, and take full ownership of the amazing new possibilities that lie ahead of us, as our values shift. If you dream about starting that

152 | *Self-Confidence Workbook for Women*

business in the suburbs but find yourself stuck in the comfort zone of your current job in the city, it will be unsettling to stick to the job without fully exploring the new shift in values and purpose. You will experience the flatness of choosing the old, familiar comfort zone over the new inspiring dream of starting your own business.

This is the plateau you reach in midlife. It is the area of your comfort zone. In this plateau, you will be searching for new meanings. Until you are ready to get unstuck life will feel mundane, dull, and uninspiring. In most cases, it does come down to lacking confidence to close the gap between the new midlife dream and reality. Holding a new value or dream in your heart while remaining stuck in an old familiar place because you lack confidence will create psychological discomfort thus diminishing your feelings of being successful.

Here's a reality check: What worked in the past to make you feel successful and accomplished as an individual may not bring you the same results of fulfillment in midlife. If this is true for you, see that as a sign to move confidently towards closing that gap between your new values and your current lifestyle.

The Link Between Conflicting Values and True Happiness

When your new values clash with your current lifestyle, it does create a feeling of not being fulfilled anymore or a feeling of lack. Your life will still look the same to you, however, your level of satisfaction and happiness is no longer defined by the old values, and therefore your life will not feel the same anymore. When you wake up in the morning, going to work to earn a living, it may no longer feel relevant or interesting because of an inner shift in values that is taking place. Clashing values result in more feelings of inadequacy, and a yearning to find new meaning in life. You must respond to the inner shifts taking place in midlife, and start recreating a life for yourself based on your changing value system.

Marcee A Martin | **153**

That yearning will only be fulfilled once you are able to fully subscribe to your new values and inner calling. This is an absolutely natural process of growing and expanding to reach a space within yourself called self-actualization. Once we conquer and reach our goals that are created from a source of inspiration within, we may need to re-examine them again when we start feeling restless, unmotivated, and simply stuck on a plateau. Confidence is key to moving again towards the new values.

You cannot hold a new value in your heart while living a life that is not congruent with that value, and find happiness or experience fulfillment. Once values shift, our life takes on new meaning based on the fulfillment of those new values. To transition successfully to support the inner shift that is taking place it is important to start making relevant adjustments in your life that lead to the fulfillment of the new values. In other words, you must start making changes in your life that directly correspond to your new midlife values.

This is the magic formula to finding true and lasting happiness during midlife: Your aim is and always has been at a subconscious level, to have a life that fully upholds all of your values. Your life is and always will be a reflection of the values that are important to you. You are always living according to your values! However, if you are feeling unfulfilled it may be due to a shift of values taking place within you.

Let's start contemplating how your values may have shifted as you began transitioning to midlife. Think of your current lifestyle, work, education, spiritual, vocational, and relationship values, and make a note of shifts that have taken place in these areas of your life since reaching midlife.

Marcee A Martin | **155**

Organizing Your Values

Your values are your roadmap to achieving success. It has always been your roadmap for success. We measure success, according to what it means to us at an individual level. The last thing you need as you go through midlife changes is to busy yourself with fantasies of success based on anyone else's expectations of you or ideas of what success ought to look like in midlife. Having confidence in yourself includes defining what success means to you, and YOU alone. After all, you are done with all the bullshit now, and life does take its own new meaning as you emerge free from shattered illusions and broken dreams of the past.

It is time to create a new roadmap for your midlife journey based on your new shifting values. You may ask why it is relevant to pay so much attention to values. The truth is that you always lived your life according to your own values whether you were consciously aware of it or not. Becoming more conscious of those values will help you to eliminate those things in your life that have become meaningless in midlife. Sometimes we hold on to doing this from the past more out of habit than expressing meaning and finding fulfillment.

Things that have diminished in value to us over the years have become redundant and should fall by the wayside. This is the comfort zone. When we do things out of familiarity and not because it brings us fulfillment anymore. Life is flat here. Everything that one does, and commits to in life is based on a set of values that expresses itself in the order of importance to you as an individual. Your values are expressed in your actions. If you place a high value on painting for example, then most likely you will be spending most of your time painting to feel fulfilled.

When Values Don't Match Anymore

However, if you have a high value on painting in your heart but you are working in a full-time office job, your true high value is therefore the job and not painting because that is how you are spending most of your

156 | *Self-Confidence Workbook for Women*

time. Painting may therefore fall below the job in the office as a second or third high value. Your life is organized in accordance with your set of values, in a hierarchy of what are the most important things to you, to the least important. You are consistently expressing your values in a hierarchy of your choice in the action that you take each day.

If you spend more time working in an office to earn a living, that job will be your highest value If you spend less time cooking it will be one of your lower values. However, if you do spend more time painting than cooking, then painting will hold a higher value for you. When we hold a value in our heart that feels more important than how we spend our time, then we experience psychological discomfort because how we are spending our time is not congruent with our true values anymore. It may have been, but since a shift has occurred it is no longer a true reflection of your new road map. When this happens it also means that we must change the way that we translate our values into the action we take so they follow the inner roadmap that we keep adjusting to reflect what is most important to us. to what is least important to us.

Let's look into your current top values: Write down your values as they appear now based on the expression of your current situation, then rearrange them according to your new values. This will give you a roadmap to your high priorities according to the hierarchy of your new values. The results will rearrange the values according to the changes you wish to manifest in midlife.

	Your Current Top Values	New Hierarchy of Values at Midlife
1.		
2.		
3.		
4.		
5.		
6.		

7.		
8.		
9.		
10.		
11.		
12.		
13.		
14.		
15.		
16.		
17.		
18.		
19.		
20.		

Key Takeaways

- The power of changing your life lies in the quality of your thoughts and self-belief.

- We may not even be consciously aware of how our thoughts can pull us down.

- Flipping the internal switch from negative to positive retrains your subconscious mind to stay on its cause.

- Everything we think about and feel we bring about.

- Recognize those triggers that bring back unpleasant memories from the past and flip the inner dialogue from negative to positive.

- When we reach midlife we have powerful new realizations and this, in turn, shifts the goalpost for us in so many ways.

- Our values naturally shift as do our beliefs based on the lessons we've learned and our growing experience.

- Determining what your new values are as you transition to your midlife years, is an important stepping stone to realizing your new purpose.

- What worked in the past to make you feel successful and accomplished as an individual may not bring you the same results of fulfillment in midlife.

- When your new values clash with your current lifestyle, it does create a feeling of not being fulfilled anymore or a feeling of lack.

In the next Chapter, you will explore your spirituality which is closely related to Universal Laws. Discover how to harness your energetic frequency by choosing thoughts that relate directly to all that you want to manifest in your life.

CHAPTER 8

WORKSHEET TO IMPROVE YOUR PURPOSE AND PERSONAL POWER

Personal power is all about exuding a level of confidence that will naturally transcend all limitations within you, and outside of you. –Marcee A Martin

That Revisited Integrity

Your level of personal confidence is also aligned to your level of integrity. It is the stamp that says "This is what I believe in and stand for as a woman of integrity." Since Carole turned 50 she's been embracing her own integrity and gray hair, making the best of honoring her new midlife journey on her own terms. Integrity can mean different things to different people. For some, it is about moral virtues and ensuring that their social values do not clash with their choices. For others, it is about simply being who they are authentically, unapologetically, and unafraid of what anyone else thinks of them. Integrity can mean total liberation when we align our values, beliefs, and lives to manifest spectacular results. Carole decided to live according to her own values and integrity and she has stopped dying her hair. She also started modeling in France, and she says she's become a different person since embracing her gray locks and midlife years.

Carole experienced real liberation when she did a simple thing as refusing to dye her hair. That is her integrity as a midlife woman wanting to be free and natural at the same time. This one small act has made her a modeling sensation and boosted her self-confidence. She also has more free time these days. The mother of four is enjoying a new round of independence as her children are all growing up. Her Instagram time is dedicated to giving other 50-plus-year-olds confidence. The biggest growth for Carole's arrival at 50 was letting go of her complexes about herself. This is her integrity today, just embracing herself fully, regardless of the external signs of aging. This is nature, always beautiful in how it expresses beauty at every age.

In her own words, "Everything I do, I do it for myself without worrying about the dictates of society or the judgment of others." The foundation of her midlife years is maintaining good health, and being sporty. She doesn't consume alcohol nor does she smoke. Eating balanced meals is important to Carole and she is a big believer in taking care of her skin too. Carole follows the rulebook to live and feel great from the inside out, drinking lots of water, eating well, exercising, and protecting herself from the harsh rays of the sun.

There are plenty of wonderful products in the market for women to stay healthy and take care of nourishing themselves. Staying beautiful, and looking radiant is a matter of maintaining an inner sense of confidence and integrity with nature. Being a little selfish to take her of herself is something that Carole enjoys. According to her, it is important for women to detach themselves from cliches associated with aging. Making self-time for some indulgences and caring for her body and mind is all part of her way of embracing her midlife years. (Gupwell, 2023)

Ask yourself: What are some things in your midlife years that you need to make peace with, to come to terms with? Does Carole's story inspire you to come to terms with external signs of aging?

Marcee A Martin | **163**

Achieving Peace of Mind

Earlier I playfully introduced you to my positivity spell, in Chapter 1. It is not hocus pocus as you would've conjured up in your imagination when first coming across the word, "spell." In fact, manifesting outcomes are consciously created first in our minds. Manifestation as an act of magic is therefore linked to enhancing our sense of wellness, and wholeness. We do have the power within to create specific outcomes that will positively impact our lives, just as J.K. Rowling achieved with her Harry Potter magical series of adventures.

Spirituality means different things to different people. For those who are religious, spirituality is about believing in a power greater than themselves. Their belief, therefore, extends to a powerful being of love, and compassion, a source of creation. Prayer is used as a kind of magical, spiritual connection in the context of religion. Faith helps people achieve their goals. Similarly, those who subscribe to achieving spirituality through meditation and other practices aimed at improving their sense inner-peace, use creative visualization techniques and meditative awakenings to manifest their soulful purpose or inner inspirational visions.

There are many wonderful, guided meditations available today on YouTube to assist you with all sorts of mental health issues. Neuroscientists have further managed to demystify spirituality by linking the benefits of meditation and even yoga to improved mental health, lower stress, and achieve clarity of purpose and vision. Neuroscientists themselves encourage meditation as an important method of creating mental pictures to help the brain function better, especially the prefrontal cortex of the brain. It is this part of the brain that is responsible for planning, memory, and executing goals successfully. Therefore spirituality today is also linked to strengthening the mind and helping the brain to function better in everyday life.

We need spirituality and wellness to bring us inner peace, and meditation might be a great place to start exploring your own spirituality. Regardless of whether you follow a specific religion or not meditation will have the same positive benefits for your body, mind, and soul. It is the inner life that we also touch during meditation that leaves a lasting healing imprint in our minds that helps us to remain resilient, and hopeful. This is the essence of what is believed to be the spirit within that resides in the body. The connection between body, mind, and soul remains a topic of deep fascination. In our quest to know and understand ourselves, we must reach deeper within.

Think about this deeply: How many times in your life did you discover that following your inner intuition may have saved you from making bigger mistakes in your life or even led you down a curious rabbit hole of greater self-discovery?

Explore Your Spirituality

From a spiritual perspective, the Universe is a magnificent forcefield of energy that we can connect with to synchronously bring about the expected results we desire in the physical world of possibilities. Our thoughts, feelings, and emotions create a vibrational frequency that leads to synchronous outcomes. The more natural our confidence levels are the greater synchronicities we can encounter in our journey. From a spiritual perspective age is relative to time, and Earth time is also relatable only to our physical existence. At a spiritual level, we are ageless, timeless, and powerful beings of light and creativity.

Pause to reflect: Let's take a moment to pause and reflect on what spirituality means to you as an individual. Are you able to tap into a much richer inner world to find new meaning and purpose in midlife?

Marcee A Martin | 167

The Initial Stages of Creating and Manifesting Our Experiences

Thoughts are powerful vibrations of possibility that we create. At any moment in our life, we can use thought to create different possibilities. We can also use thought to create vibrations in the Universe that resonate with a much grander vision to enrich us more spiritually. This is exactly how some of the great spiritual entities manifest their magic in the world. They project their creative thoughts into the Universe and meditate on those visions to bring about their powerful manifestation, through a series of actions that follow, inspired from within during their cosmic encounters.

Thought is a powerful way that we begin the journey of creation, consciously or unconsciously. When we constantly entertain negative, self-defeating thoughts we are in fact setting in motion action that will correspond with those thoughts. If those negative thoughts become embedded into our subconscious minds as factual beliefs about ourselves, we will continue to project that "negative truth" to the external world, consciously or unconsciously.

When we manifest out of fear we are doing so unconsciously. Sadly, this in turn attracts more negative experiences than positive ones. From a spiritual perspective, the Universe is an entity that exists by a set of laws. When we are consciously aware of the laws of the Universe, we will be able to match our responses and choices accordingly to produce great results in all areas of our life. The Universal laws have been observed and studied over many centuries by spiritual masters, and some of them are also revealed in some of the major religions of the world.

The Universe also registers thoughts as an energetic extension of your supernatural presence. Thoughts are also vibrational energy that we emit when we tune into them consciously. The lower vibrational thoughts we emit, such as fear, self-doubt, self-criticism, and self-hate bring us down, as their vibrational energy is dense, negative, and draining. Higher thoughts that are more uplifting, positive, and inspirational have

168 | *Self-Confidence Workbook for Women*

higher frequencies and they, in turn, elevate our moods and open up both heart and mind to greater possibilities.

Let's Aim To Improve Our Vibrational Frequency

We must therefore strive to have more high-vibrational experiences as this in turn will boost our level of confidence. From a purely spiritual perspective, positive, more uplifting thoughts align beautifully with higher, more supportive frequencies in the Universe. They also correspond to the true nature of your soul, which is lighter than darkness. The dark thoughts associated with negativity and fear are therefore dense, ego-driven thoughts derived from unrealistic low expectations of ourselves. When we choose to react negatively to experiences, challenges, and situations, we naturally feel very downcast.

This vibrational frequency is also what we emit, making it harder to break away from the dark spells we put ourselves under when we persist with negative thoughts. However, you can shift to higher frequencies. Self-care also helps us to shift our energy. This is also another reason daily self-care is a fundamental part of our journey back to psychological health and wellness. When you neglect self-care it also makes it harder to get back to positive more easily and dismiss the negative vibes. Self-care is a great way of staying in touch with our daily needs and it provides a great outlet for stress and pent-up negativity. You can therefore think of self-care as an important way of connecting more positively to ourselves, and the Universe!

The Universal Laws That Regulate Life in the Best Way

The Law of Attraction

The law of attraction corresponds greatly with the law of cause and effect. Once again from a neuroscientific perspective this law as well as the other Universal Laws which many of the main religions also promulgate can be understood by the manner in which the brain also works. As you think so shall you be! Everything that you desire,

Marcee A Martin | **169**

according to this magnificent law, is within your reach. Attracting it to you requires more than wishful thinking. While thought itself is powerful to bring you what you need at times, at other times more effort may be required on your part.

The basic premise of this law is that like attracts likes. Also, whatever is inside of you that you desire can be manifested on the basis of this law. Belief is central to the effectiveness of the law of attraction. You must believe in your desire, and want it. It is also important to vibrate at a frequency of your desired intention. Therefore let your thoughts focus on the outcome that you wish to manifest. When you flip that internal switch of inner dialogue to a more positive frequency your chances of manifesting at that frequency also improve. Taking action is also an important part of manifestation. The Universe also applauds action. (Reagan, 2020)

The Law of Concentration

This law is a sub-law of the Law of Cause and Effect. According to it, whatever you give energy to will grow and expand in proportion to the effort or energy you direct toward those things. Whether it is related to some thought or action that is either positive or negative the law is still applicable. This is also why human behavior experts encourage the nurturing of persistence, resilience, and determination. The greater your effort the greater will be your rewards. If you decide to nurture more negative thoughts that relate to your fears, as well as self-defeating limiting beliefs, you will manifest more of these, less successful, and positively inspired ideas, thoughts, and beliefs. Success belongs to those who persist and who believe in their ideas, goals, and vision. (Sinrich, 2015)

The Law of Correspondence

According to this law, what goes around comes around. In other words, as you sow shall you reap. Our reality is a mirror of patterns of what is happening inside of us. It also reflects patterns corresponding in the Universe which is where the study of cosmology becomes relevant in our lives. "As above, so below. As within, so without." If your life is chaotic and riddled with worry, anxiety, and fear this can easily manifest externally in your world. We must therefore consciously strive to improve the quality of our inner life, to reap rewards in the manner in which it is reflected in our outer lives.

The Law of Correspondence calls us to heal and nurture more loving thoughts about ourselves. It also calls us to examine the quality of life we feel deserving of. When we feel more deserving of love, it will correspond to what we receive. Any deficiency you feel will correspond with how other people receive your signal, which is the vibration you are emitting based on your thoughts, feelings, emotions, and beliefs. To attract abundance, you must therefore feel abundant from within. (Reagan, 2020)

The Law of Substitution

According to this law it is impossible to drop a thought completely. Therefore, if you find yourself having a negative thought more often than not about something or quality about yourself, instead of focusing on your strengths, you can decide NOT to have any more of those negative thoughts. You also need to replace those thoughts with better, more positive ones instead of just dropping them altogether because they won't just go away easily, as we already know. From a neuroscientific perspective, replacing negative thoughts with more positive ones is how we can train our minds to accept new truths about ourselves. Instead of repeatedly saying to yourself, that you will never get back the figure you enjoyed in your twenties, change it to, "I love and honor my health and body. Right now I am perfectly healthy and happy."

Everything that you say repeatedly to your subconscious mind becomes a habit, and an ingrained way of thinking and behaving. From this perspective, it does make sense to replace or substitute negative thoughts with more positive ones. This is also relatable to how the subconscious mind works. Unless we consciously change our thoughts and thinking patterns, the former ones will remain in control. It makes sense to commit to flipping the switch of your internal dialogue from negative to positive to completely rewire your brain and your subconscious mind. So instead of deciding not to say to yourself negative things, commit to replacing those thoughts with positive affirmations. (Wesson, 2012)

The Law of Emotion

According to this law, our emotions can give us a clue to directing change in our lives to address issues that our emotions bring up for us. Instead of being at the mercy of every emotion we encounter, we can use them to direct change to neutralize strong emotions and reverse any negative side effects related to those emotions. Every thought is a vibration, and it is thoughts that create feelings and emotions. The strength of our thoughts and feelings, therefore, results in the strength of those corresponding emotions. Since all emotions create vibrational energy, we are bound to be impacted negatively or positively by the corresponding vibration which will in turn manifest into experiences, thoughts, and synchronicities in our lives.

We can direct the quality of our inner world based on the quality of the emotions we encounter. When strong emotions start controlling our behavior then it can throw both our inner and outer worlds into chaos. Our aim should be to neutralize strong emotions to bring about meaningful change in our lives from within, and to seek resolutions aimed at improving our mental health. This will ultimately have a profound impact on what we manifest in our lives. (Understanding Emotions, n.d.)

Power of Decision

It was Lao Tzu who once said that the journey of a thousand miles begins with one small step. The decisions that we make whether small or large, good, or bad, negative or positive takes us in new directions, and is an expression of our free will. Therefore it is important for us to constantly question the quality of the decisions we make, to ascertain the desired results based on our expectations.

We must also ask ourselves whether these decisions are congruent with our level of integrity and values, as ultimately we must aim for this, to achieve lasting happiness and fulfillment. The power of our decisions will impact our lives and will also correlate to the Universal laws that determine what we are consistently attracting in our lives.

Pause to reflect on how the Universal laws are impacting your life at present, based on your choices. Also, reflect on what you can do now to improve the results you wish to manifest. Write down your insights in the space provided below.

174 | *Self-Confidence Workbook for Women*

It's Only Fear That May Be Holding You Back

As you can see from our insightful discussions above it is only fear and negativity that are ultimately holding you back from realizing your fullest potential. Fear is only powerful when you believe it to be true. Once it sets in and takes over our lives it can keep us stuck in one place for a long time thus robbing us of our natural sense of curiosity to explore new domains of potential within ourselves. It is not difficult to transcend fear. It is as easy as flipping the switch from fear to love.

The opposite of fear is love. Choosing love over fear will help you to transcend doubt, anxiety, and negativity. Always ask yourself what is the worst that could happen if you give something your best shot. The worst is that you may fail in your effort, and the absolute worst is that you keep failing with every effort until you finally win. Every failure is a lesson. Just keep moving forward and if you are determined enough and apply Universal laws precisely there is no reason you can't succeed!

How is fear holding you back now in midlife, and what can you do today to flip that switch from fear to love? In which areas of your life is fear dictating the outcome before you've actually even tried to achieve a different result?

Marcee A Martin | 175

176 | *Self-Confidence Workbook for Women*

Key Takeaways

- Your level of personal confidence is also aligned with your level of integrity.

- We do have the power within to create specific outcomes that will positively impact our lives.

- Neuroscientists have demystified spirituality by linking the benefits of meditation and the practice of yoga to improved mental health, lower stress, and clarity of purpose, vision, and goals.

- The Universe also reacts to all vibrational energy according to its projection to bring forth the experiences that we are seeking.

- Our thoughts, feelings, and emotions create a vibrational frequency that leads to synchronous outcomes.

- According to the law of attraction, everything that you desire is within your reach.

- The law of correspondence works when you give energy to those things that you desire to manifest.

- According to the law of substitution, it is impossible to drop a thought completely. We must replace them.

- Our emotions can give us a clue as to where in our lives we must direct change, starting in our thoughts.

- The decisions that we make whether small or large, good, or bad, negative or positive takes us in new directions, and is an expression of our free will.

In the next Chapter, we will embrace powerful tools to achieve self-mastery!

CHAPTER 9

COMPETENCE AND PERSONAL MASTERY

Everything that you need to succeed is right within you.
—Marcee A Martin

What Is the Limit

There is no limit to what you can achieve at any age. Everything and anything is possible. All you need to do is surround yourself with inspiration, set a clear blueprint for what you want to achieve, then go out with full force and enthusiasm to manifest what you desire to achieve. Everything that you are capable of achieving starts and ends in the mind. If it is inspiration that you are searching for outside yourself, the internet is a great place to start looking. There are many insightful stories of brave women who have over the centuries since the beginning of creation withstood great challenges to achieve greatness. These women were trailblazers in their own right, not because they wanted to be famous, but because they all believed in something greater than themselves. It started out in the shape of thoughts, ideas, and inspiration and manifested in great achievements, making history in some cases.

Marie Marvingt is one such trailblazer who continued making history throughout her life regardless of her age or societal limitations during her lifetime. She was the first woman to get her pilot's license for flying a hot balloon, a gold medalist champion in all sports, the inventor of the flying ambulance service, the first woman to fly a plane during world war 1, and at the age of 86 she cycled 175 miles from Nancy to Paris. She was unstoppable at every age of her life! If you trace her entire life, you'll be amazed at her achievements which included training wild animals in a circus. The limit that you set for yourself really depends on you, and how far you are willing to go to feel fulfilled by your achievements. You must believe that anything can happen at any time that will change the course of your life.

Inspiration Like Lightning Strikes Unannounced

Inspiration can strike at any time, and if you are already flowing with positivity, confidence, and healthy self-esteem, you will be able to recognize inspiration when it shows up in your life. Sometimes the best of your plans may not manifest exactly as you want them to. Thankfully when synchronicity shows up in your life, it can take your best plans to new levels of inspiration beyond your wildest dreams! How your destiny is shaped is also dependent on the quality of thoughts you entertain about yourself, as well as your willingness to achieve fulfillment in your life. Remember what success means to you will not be the same as what success means for everybody else.

J.K. Rowling was writing adult novels, when out of the blue while sitting on a train that was delayed, inspiration struck creating her bestselling fantastical Harry Potter series. Synchronicity always shows up in everyone's life when the time is right. Meditation and mindfulness also increase your chances of recognizing synchronicity when it arrives with Universal clues and clear signs of what your next best move should be. You need to be confident enough to trust your intuition and to recognize the signs the Universe is showing you.

Designing Your Ideal Work-Life

Achieving real success according to how YOU define success is key to living a full, and meaningful life. One of the biggest changes that women experience in midlife, is redefining what success means to them. Making a career change is a common midlife goal for many women, as they begin redefining what is working and what isn't working for them career-wise. As we discussed earlier in Chapter 7, your values are constantly changing as you expand and grow in areas of interest. Sometimes we may completely outgrow old values and take on new careers! Embrace this if it is your journey, and remember that everything is possible, one step at a time!

This is why it is important when you realize that your values are shifting to sit down with pen and paper and get very clear, deliberately clear, about what success looks like to you now. This in turn will remove any confusion or inner conflict between what was important to you in the past and what is important to you now. It will seem strange to own up to your shifting values at first. However, in time, and once you give yourself permission to embrace change, it will be a journey that you will look forward to taking. Change is as good as an exotic holiday, full of possibility, without knowing what your next experience will be or feel like.

Having a plan in place and fully articulating your new midlife vision on paper will help to concretize your ideas. Breathing life into your vision by acknowledging what you want, is the first foundation you will be creating for your new life. It will also help your brain to construct a clear frame of reference and plan of action to support your new efforts. Just as the Eiffel Tower needed a blueprint in place before the construction began, so do you, to ensure that you are developing it one step at a time, and strategically giving it the attention it requires to ensure success. Here are some of the critical steps to fulfill as you begin to breathe life into your vision on paper.

Marcee A Martin | **181**

Articulate Your Vision in Broad Strokes

Express to yourself verbally, the life you envisage for yourself according to your new values, and feel free to go into as much detail as possible. If you like, you can start a video diary to express yourself and record your vision and dreams for the near future. Get it all out of your system, and let go of the fear associated with the anticipated change or the discomfort you may feel at first. Express yourself fully from your heart. This video is just for you! Once you've done that, write down here the main points of your new expanding vision.

1.	
2.	
3.	
4.	
5.	
6.	
7.	
8.	
9.	
10.	
11.	
12.	
13.	
14.	
15.	
16.	
17.	
18.	
19.	
20.	

Identify Your New Interests and Areas of Excellence

Break down the new interests into bit-sized goals, and get a bit more detailed as you strategically assess new areas for learning opportunities. At the same time make a list of your current areas of excellence and also identify ways in which you can raise the bar higher, to ensure that your areas of excellence remain market related. Convert those areas of excellence into new opportunities that might be worth exploring. Even though your values have shifted there might be opportunities to still capitalize on areas of excellence to create new business opportunities for yourself.

No.	New Areas of Interest	Areas of Excellence
1.		
2.		
3.		
4.		
5.		
6.		
7.		
8.		
9.		
10.		
11.		
12.		
13.		
14.		
15.		
16.		
17.		

18.	
19.	
20.	

Identify the Goals You Want to Achieve Over the Next 5–10 Years

Consider what you would love to achieve over the next 5–10 years of your life. Keep your list as detailed as possible. Also, keep in mind the vision that you articulated and begin with the end in mind. Be very specific and paint a clear picture of what your life will look like in all areas listed below. If your financial goal is to earn a seven-figure income, then articulate clearly how you intend to earn that figure. If you don't have all the answers as yet, that is okay. This exercise is to get you thinking more long-term to start moving in that direction.

- Career
- Finance
- Love
- Family
- Health & Wellness
- Spiritual
- Education

Marcee A Martin | **185**

Tips to Stay on the Path of Your Goals

Break down your goals.	Break down your goals into smaller chunks. Remember that you cannot eat the elephant all at once!
Celebrate the milestones.	As you achieve smaller goals, celebrate the milestones along the way!
Reward yourself.	Don't hold back from rewarding yourself for all the effort you're making along the way! As you achieve one bite-sized goal at a time, reward yourself.
Embrace baby steps.	Don't feel overwhelmed by the enormity of your vision. Take things one baby step at a time.
Visualize your goals often.	Stay congruent with your vision, and visualize it like a movie in your mind as you read through your goals.
Get organized and be systematic in your approach.	Create your own systems to ensure that you are on track with your goals, and be organized by prioritizing tasks each day.
Keep your goals in sight	Create a vision board and place it where you can regularly see the list of your goals. You can also store one on your computer in the format of slides. Include pictures and short sentences of motivation.
Surround yourself with positive people and vibes.	Keep yourself inspired by enjoying the company of positive like-minded people.
Talk to your partner.	If you are in a relationship, communicate often with your partner about your goals and your progress.

186 | *Self-Confidence Workbook for Women*

Take regular breaks for hobbies.	Make sure to get some social and rest time in between working on your goals to do other things that you love, and to also rejuvenate yourself.
Think of the amazing results on the way!	Keep yourself motivated by thinking of how your hard work will pay off!
Avoid Procrastination.	Delayed action is delayed results!
Acknowledge that you can't control everything.	Things are bound to go wrong and not always work out in your favor at times. Don't resist it. Accept failure and keep moving forward, looking ahead!

Key Takeaways

- There is no limit to what you can achieve at any age.
- Everything that you are capable of achieving starts and ends in the mind.
- The limit that you set for yourself really depends on you, and how far you are willing to go to feel fulfilled by your achievements.
- Inspiration can strike at any time.
- Always be open-minded and willing to explore new possibilities.
- Be unstoppable in your quest to achieve personal fulfillment.
- Sometimes the best of your plans may not manifest exactly as you want them to.
- Self-esteem is your opinion of yourself.
- Always ask yourself: How good is my opinion of myself today?
- If you have a good opinion of yourself, you will have healthy self-esteem.

- Persistent negative thinking about yourself can also result in you having a low opinion of yourself.
- Identify and challenge your negative beliefs about yourself and your capabilities.
- Achieving real success according to how YOU define success is key to living a full, and meaningful life.
- It is important to have a plan in place for at least the next 5–10 years of your life.

CHAPTER 10

WORKING WITH THE DEEP GAME OF SELF-CONFIDENCE

Little bursts of inspiration throughout the day can uplift your spirit and get you through anything. Don't ever give up on yourself! –Marcee A Martin

The Law of Belief

Earlier when we started our journey together in this book, I asked you an important self-reflective question. When you look in the mirror what do you see in yourself? It is important to just let your answers flow naturally as it will reveal some truths and some limited beliefs that you may still be holding onto. Write it down here so we can look deeper into this when we next discuss the law of belief.

_____
_____
_____
_____

190 | *Self-Confidence Workbook for Women*

The law of belief simply states that we hold in our minds what we believe to be true about ourselves. In other words, life gives us what we feel and believe, and not necessarily what we want. Unless what we feel and believe is closely aligned with what we want, we will not achieve everything precisely as we desire. It is a simple law to get. This is the magic that self-belief holds for us. When you apply this law it is a matter of convincing your mind that you already believe in the things that you desire to have. However, it is also true that you must feel deserving of achieving what you want, and you must persevere, and keep moving towards it.

To really get the most out of this law, personal transformation becomes more profound when you see so much more in yourself than you are currently exploring. What we see in the mirror is a reflection of the choices we've made to date based on our expectations, and personal beliefs. It is still not the complete picture. To change what you see in the mirror requires complete acceptance of the image that greets you in your mind, and acknowledgment that you are always deserving of more. Examining your setbacks, and going deeper to understand how you can turn them around includes removing limitations that we have created for ourselves.

Ask yourself now: How can I turn around the setbacks that I am currently facing and are my expectations realistic?

192 | *Self-Confidence Workbook for Women*

It is important to start setting small realistic and achievable expectations of yourself. This will boost your level of confidence and increase your self-belief. When we set small, incremental but meaningful expectations, we regain confidence as soon as we start achieving them. Once this momentum keeps expanding, our confidence levels also expand simultaneously, thus also enabling us to feel more accepting of ourselves and more hopeful about our current situation. It is then that we can learn to cope better with our midlife journey. Understanding that acceptance, self-belief, and committing to realistic goals and expectations is a consistent way of increasing self-confidence, will move you in the direction of improving the overall quality of your life. One magical step forward at a time, all adds up to amazing results. Keep embracing the magic of tiny steps.

Being Your Own Cheerleader Increases Your Self-Belief

Here are some wonderful tips on how you can improve how you feel about yourself. Remember how important and vibrant it was to have cheerleaders in high school on the sports team? It really did make a team stand out strongly. It brought some color and more excitement to the sports field and it built team morale! Well, you can be your own cheerleader when you need support to level up your own game in life. Life is not static. It has its ups and downs. Keep cheering yourself onwards and you will make the mark! Here's how you can be your own cheerleader:

- **Control your mental pictures:** Instead of seeing yourself as someone who is always failing, stumbling, or not being able to handle too much pressure, turn it around and start seeing yourself as always succeeding, always winning in life. See yourself achieving the success that you truly want, and use that to shape your outer reality. Use creative visualization when you meditate to increase your chances of success. Build on the mental pictures in your mind that you wish to manifest daily and keep moving forward in that direction.

Marcee A Martin | **193**

- **Develop discipline and courage:** Create a routine of discipline that moves you forward productively. Fulfill your highest priorities each day, and cheer yourself on when it gets tough. See yourself succeeding in each of your daily tasks and remind yourself consistently why it is important to achieve your high-priority actions each and every day!

- **Take excellent care of yourself:** Self-care should always be one of the priority routines that you follow daily. When things get tough, maintain your self-care routine. It will give you the extra energy boost that you need. It is easy to fall into self-neglect when things are not going your way. That will only worsen how you feel about yourself. Cheer yourself on, to do more to ensure that you are always shining your light from the inside out. It will help you cope better with stressful situations when they appear in your life. You will be better equipped spiritually, psychologically, and mentally when you apply self-care daily.

- **Apply the power of positive self-talk:** How you communicate with yourself remains vitally important. Start eliminating negative self-talk from your life. Remind yourself that just as it's easy to think negative things about yourself, it is easy to start thinking positive things about yourself. The moment you catch yourself getting caught in negative self-talk, flip that switch to being more optimistic about your life. Just press STOP. Then change the self-talk to being more positive and uplifting. Instead of saying to yourself that you can't, say that you can! Instead of pulling yourself down, uplift yourself regardless of the situation, and have a firm grip on the situation to turn it around. You have the power within you to achieve greatness each and every day of your life.

Developing Strength and Resilience

If we allow every setback to bring us to our knees, anxiety, depression, and chronic stress will take over and destroy all the good that you are building right now. Developing healthy coping skills is essential. We know already that life gets tough, and that how we deal with challenges will ultimately determine the quality of the results of our efforts. You are built to last and it is your natural birthright to seek more enjoyment. Resilience can be developed if you find that you are struggling at times. It is natural to sweat when things get tough. It is also easy to flip that switch from negative to positive and choose ways to cope better. Choose the last option! An attitude of gratitude can shift your perspective dramatically.

Tips to Improve Your Resilience

- **Get connected:** Build strong, resilient, positive, relationships with people, and always maintain them. We need each other to strengthen ourselves and offer mutual encouragement. So don't be afraid to connect with others, more so when things appear to be more challenging. Reach out for support from positively inspiring people, and those who you love and trust. Avoid maintaining relations with people who are not sincere or trustworthy. Toxic relationships just add to the list of stressful things to cope with.

- **Make every day count:** Set out deliberately to make each and every day meaningful for you. Put your needs at the center of your agenda, and ensure that your time is occupied with activities that are of value to you. Stick to your goals and never stop learning.

- **Learn from all experiences:** We can only keep learning and growing from all experiences. You've come this far. Here you are at midlife. You've had to cope with a lot over the years. You're still here, and you are going to rock this journey too with your newfound goals, and confidence just as I am doing in my life. As you examine your life's lessons, adapt accordingly. Develop new coping strategies, and make resolutions that will keep the darkness out of your life. We are here to learn, love, grow, and expand, and you're still here ready to do more amazing things with your life.

- **Always remain hopeful:** You already know from the past, that hope is the seed of a better tomorrow. So don't give up on yourself when things get tough. Keep your chin up and believe that things will turn around. When you give up, you limit your possibilities, but

Marcee A Martin | **195**

when you harness your skills and remain optimistic while staring straight into the face of adversity, you are continuously opening new doors to greater possibilities.

- **Be Proactive always:** Stay one step ahead of the game. Pay attention to your problems, and issues as they arise, and keep taking positive action to find healthy solutions. Also, be kind to yourself, and anticipate your next move in accordance with experiences, setbacks, and opportunities. Being proactive also includes taking care of YOU continuously, to ensure that your mental, psychological, and spiritual health does not suffer.

Let's take some time to count our blessings and start planting the seeds of hope right now. Write down what your blessings are (all of them), and in the next column, let's explore the reasons why we are hopeful. As we conclude our amazing journey in this book, I encourage you to always strive to be more hopeful, optimistic, and abundant in your approach to life!

Count Your Blessings	Planting the Seeds of Hope

Key Takeaways

- The law of belief simply states that we hold in our minds what we believe to be true about ourselves.

- When you apply this law it is a matter of convincing your mind that you already believe in the things that you desire to have.

- What we see in the mirror is a reflection of the choices we've made to date, based on our expectations, and personal beliefs.

- Accepting accountability of those choices will bring you inner-peace, and help you to move away from regret.

- We can't change the past, but we can make changes now by learning lessons from the past.

- Focus on your strengths and picture winning in life.

- You can turn every setback into a comeback when you adopt a positive outlook and attitude.

- Create a routine of discipline that moves you forward productively.

- You are built to last and it is your natural birthright to seek more enjoyment.

- It is natural to sweat when things get tough. Be kind to yourself always!

- Pay attention to your issues as they arise, and keep taking positive action to find healthy solutions.
- Adopt an attitude of gratitude by counting your blessings often.
- Set out deliberately to make each and every day meaningful for you.

CONCLUSION

The benefits of reaching midlife far outshine the challenges associated with approaching or reaching menopause. Whether you are in your 40s or past your 60s life can keep getting better and more fulfilling as long as you decide to keep doing the things that you love! It is about adopting the right attitude, one that pays more attention to the gains and less attention to the losses. After all, as you've just discovered in our journey together, everything that happens on the outside is a matter of perception, reaction, and attitude. Of course, we also know that SH*T happens to the best of us, and we can own it by learning from it! At midlife, a woman truly knows herself and she is more capable than she ever was in the past to ensure more enduring happiness.

When I walk into a room full of enthused midlife women ready to hear me speak about my own midlife transition, I see in all of them an enlightened soul, a woman who knows and understands the value of resilience, and positivity. We have come together to support each other in our ongoing midlife journey, to ensure that it does promise to be so much more than we once expected. We are here together, working to improve every level of our future experience and encounters to develop more opportunities for growth and to cultivate a new approach to being a midlife woman. That new approach depends on the level of self-confidence we feel each day, the choices we are making, and the lessons we are learning.

It is time to get more comfortable in our skins, to embrace the past without discarding our experiences or minimizing ourselves. It is time to use our strengths to improve our lives, hone our talents, and contribute powerfully. You know what you like and what you don't like, what works and what does not work for you anymore. You've done the work now to own your SH*T and you now have so much more clarity, including a new blueprint of your new values and goals. Being a badass woman means being authentically powerful, and still curious about what is coming next. It is about shedding the superficial layer of skin from our youth that kept us stuck in being more pleasing than powerful in our own right.

I also look forward to hearing from you personally. Send me an email, tell me what you think about my series, share your midlife stories, and let us connect, heal, and transform our lives together, to reflect our fullest and greatest potential. My email address again is hello@marceemartin. com. An honest review of my book will also be much appreciated: Let others know how you've benefitted, and how they can too. Thank you sincerely for taking this journey with me. Until next time, keep shining!

ABOUT THE AUTHOR

Marcee calls herself the "happiest author" on Planet Earth. However, her journey to inner happiness was long, protracted, and often complex. In the end, it was fulfilling and it led her to a quest of helping midlife women navigate their lives to new inspired destinations. After suffering from years of low self-esteem, chronic anxiety, non-existent self-confidence, and a plethora of other emotional disorders, Marcee finally turned her life around.

Her breakthrough came when she was on the brink of a total mental and emotional breakdown. She searched through more than 200 books (across several niches) for answers, and insight into finding true happiness. She also watched more than 200 videos and attended many seminars and classes. Hitting rock bottom mentally and emotionally released her inner desire to improve her life in every way possible.

The secrets of human relationships and psychology that she unearthed transformed her life and she never looked back. Her life became a series of breakthroughs until she completely rebuilt and developed a new relationship with herself—learning all about self-love. This new relationship also improved her communication skills with other people. Marcee believes that everyone can communicate better if they know how to listen to others and read their body language.

In her own words, "I was born shy but I have come to realize that with the right approach, anybody can become a great conversationalist and a people magnet. My life mission is to teach that approach." For the last five years, Marcee's new quest has been bringing other people closer

Marcee A Martin | **201**

to happiness through her books. The pillars of her teachings revolve around the following:

- Mindfulness and meditation techniques for anxiety, depression, and stress.
- The importance of listening (and not just hearing).
- Ways to challenge and fix cognitive distortions.
- The best ways to communicate even during difficult times.
- New methods to shape and discuss with your inner critic.
- CBT techniques for restoring emotional balance.
- The importance of self-love, self-esteem, and self-confidence.
- How to deepen empathetic traits without becoming codependent.
- Coaching to build conversational skills.
- Learning to develop charisma and using witty banter to great effect.
- Body language clues and how to read between the lines.

Marcee lives in New York City with her best friend (husband), and two cats!

Thanks for reading my book!

I am grateful that, from all the books on Amazon, you chose my book. It is my hope that you found great value in it.

Before you leave, can I ask a small fraction of your time? I'd like to ask you to leave me a **review on Amazon, or a star-rating**; doing so is immensely helpful for an independent author like me.

This is one way you can help me reach more people, to spread the word how this book can potentially help others.

Scan to leave a review:

$129 FREE

Achieve a Worry-Free Smile with these
12 Mental Health Books!

The Easy Way to Improve Mental Health

Therapy doesn't have to be so expensive and complicated. That's why we are giving you these 7 eBooks and 5 bonus workbooks so you can start improving your mental health right away, without leaving your home!

- **Stop Worrying All the Time**: Stop those nagging thoughts in their tracks with mindfulness and anti-anxiety tips expert CBT therapists use!

- **Do Therapy Your Way**: Start taking action with 5 BONUS workbooks, so you can start smiling, laughing, and enjoying life on your own!

- **Love Yourself, Love Others**: Enhance your career, relationships, hobbies, and more as you march through each day with confident self-esteem

Scan to download:

Loved this book? You may also want the other books in this series:

What others are saying:

Christina Forster
★★★★★ **Great book!**
Reviewed in the United States on January 31, 2023
Verified Purchase

This book is so helpful in learning about self-worth and self-esteem and different treatments to help. It was interesting reading about how self-doubt can creep in and start to cause a decrease in self-esteem and self-confidence. Certain things such as perfectionism can lead to self-doubt. I enjoyed learning more about CBT and how to use it to help with one's sense of self. CBT can help you overcome self-doubt. It is explained in a very easy to understand way. I really enjoyed the chapter on radical self-compassion. If we could all learn to be kinder to ourselves it would go a long way!

A D
★★★★★ **Improve your confidence**
Reviewed in the United States on January 30, 2023
Verified Purchase

If you are your own worst critic like me then this book can help. They provide positive psychology exercises and CBT worksheets to help you overcome your mind and silence your inner critics. You learn ways to reduce perfectionism. Explain the roots of self-doubt and provide exercises to work on understanding yourself worth. I love chapter 7 that gives exercises for radical compassion. By the end I gained useful tools to help me take more control of my life.

Daniela Hernández
★★★★★ **Healing book**
Reviewed in the United States on January 30, 2023
Verified Purchase

Unfortunately a few years ago I had a relationship that lowered my self-esteem and now I'm trying to start a new relationship with another person. However, my lack of self-esteem is affecting both of us. This book helped me heal many wounds and love myself over anything else.

Scan to check out books on Amazon

REFERENCES

Ten Steps to Develop an Abundance Mindset. (2019, September 23). Chopra. https://www.chopra.com/articles/10-steps-to-develop-an-abundance-mindset

Apter, T. (2011, August 11). Midlife Women: Why Are They More Assertive? Psychology Today. https://www.psychologytoday.com/us/blog/domestic-intelligence/201108/midlife-women-why-are-they-more-assertive

Become more Confident: The 10 Best Expert Tips for Women. (2020, October 21). PsyCat Games. https://psycatgames.com/magazine/conversation-starters/how-to-be-more-confident-for-girls/

Calayag, K. (2021, December 9). JK Rowling Net Worth: "Harry Potter" Author Among Richest 1% In The World. International Business Times. https://www.ibtimes.com/jk-rowling-net-worth-harry-potter-author-among-richest-1-world-3353706

Cherry, K. (2019). Six Psychological Strategies for Success in Life. Verywell Mind. https://www.verywellmind.com/how-to-be-successful-in-life-4165743

Cherry, K. (2022, November 7). What Are the Signs of Healthy or Low Self-Esteem? Verywell Mind. https://www.verywellmind.com/what-is-self-esteem-2795868

Cuncic, A. (2020, June 29). How to Change Your Negative Thought Patterns When You Have SAD. Verywell Mind. https://www.verywellmind.com/how-to-change-negative-thinking-3024843

Dr. John Demartini. (n.d.). Huffington Post. https://www.huffpost.com/author/dr-john-demartini

Ghosh, A. (2018, September 14). How to Stay Consistent and Realize Your Dreams. Lifehack. https://www.lifehack.org/788257/how-to-stay-consistent

Grant, K. (2013, November 28). Here Are 7 Tips On Becoming Unstoppable In Midlife. Second Half Dream Life. https://www.chooseyourbestlifenow.com/becoming-unstoppable-in-the-midlife-years/

Gupwell, K.-A. (2023, April 1). I'm more confident since I embraced my grey hair - I even became a model at 50. Dailystar.co.uk. https://www.dailystar.co.uk/real-life/im-much-more-confident-embraced-29561641

https://www.facebook.com/IQmatrix. (2009, April 13). The Universal Law of Cause and Effect and its Impact on Your Life. IQ Matrix Blog. https://blog.iqmatrix.com/law-of-cause-effect

James, A. (2017, October 27). 6 Mindfulness Exercises You Can Try Today. Pocket Mindfulness. https://www.pocketmindfulness.com/6-mindfulness-exercises-you-can-try-today/

Kirilova, K. (2019, February 19). Six Ways to Improve Your Self-image and Mindset at Midlife. Career Life Choices. https://careerlifechoices.com/your-self-image-and-mindset-at-midlife/

Kukteliones, C. (n.d.). The Power of Perspective – 9P Online. Nine Principles.

Https://9principles.com/. Retrieved April 1, 2023, from https://9principles.com/learning/the-power-of-perspective/

Martin, Dr. M. (2015, August 11). Five Ways Middle-Aged Women Can Feel More Visible. HuffPost. https://www.huffpost.com/entry/how-middle-aged-women-can-feel-more-visible_b_7927232

Menopause and your mental wellbeing. (2022, November 29). NHS. https://www.nhsinform.scot/healthy-living/womens-health/

later-years-around-50-years-and-over/menopause-and-post-menopause-health/menopause-and-your-mental-wellbeing/

Montano, D. (2020). *Confidence for women.* Kindle Publishing.

Nayar, V. (2010, July 15). *The Miracle of Making Mistakes. Harvard Business Review.* https://hbr.org/2010/07/the-miracle-of-making-mistakes

NHS. (2021, February 1). *Raising low self-esteem. NHS.* https://www.nhs.uk/mental-health/self-help/tips-and-support/raise-low-self-esteem/

Perry, M., CSCS, & CPT. (2010, October 19). *31 Reasons To Get In Shape & Exercise More. BuiltLean.* https://www.builtlean.com/31-reasons-get-in-shape-and-exercise/

Pychyl, T. (2012, April 10). *The Power of Habit. Psychology Today.* https://www.psychologytoday.com/us/blog/dont-delay/201204/the-power-habit

Reagan, S. (2020, April 16). *12 Universal Laws & How To Use Them To Unlock A More Spiritual Life. Mindbodygreen.* https://www.mindbodygreen.com/articles/the-12-universal-laws-and-how-to-practice-them

Sicinski, A. (2015, December 28). *Law of Concentration what is? MasterMind Matrix.* https://mastermindmatrix.com/knowledge-base/law-of-concentration/

Sinrich, J. (2023, February 14). *15 Stories That Prove It's Never Too Late to Change Your Life. Reader's Digest.* https://www.rd.com/list/never-too-late-change-your-life/

Taylor, J. (2009). *Sports: Introduction to Confidence. Psychology Today.* https://www.psychologytoday.com/us/blog/the-power-prime/200911/sports-introduction-confidence

Understanding Emotions with the Universal Laws. (n.d.). *Mind Your Reality.* https://www.mind-your-reality.com/understanding-emotions.html

Voll, D. (2023, March 15). *4 Steps to Identifying Your Purpose in Midlife. Sixty and Me.* https://sixtyandme.com/identify-purpose-midlife/

Wesson, C. (2012, May 6). *The Law of Substitution. Making Positive Changes.* https://www.makingpositivechanges.co.uk/the-law-of-substitution/

When Overthinking Becomes a Problem & What You Can Do About It. (n.d.). https://www.houstonmethodist.org/blog/articles/2021/apr/when-overthinking-becomes-a-problem-and-what-you-can-do-about-it/

Image References

Aianana. (2017). *Girl-beach-island-turquoise-summer-2066101. [Image]. Pixabay.* https://pixabay.com/photos/girl-beach-island-turquoise-summer-2066101/

Akyurt, E. (2018). *Sunset-woman-model-pose-yoga-3726023. [Image]. Pixabay.* https://pixabay.com/photos/sunset-woman-model-pose-yoga-3726023/

Alexa. (2017). *Face-painting-colorful-woman-2848057. [Image]. Pixabay.* https://pixabay.com/photos/face-painting-colorful-woman-2848057/

Altmann, G. (2013). *Girl-headphones-grades-treble-clef-140569. [Image]. Pixabay.* https://pixabay.com/illustrations/girl-headphones-grades-treble-clef-140569/

Altmann, G. (2018). *Never-stop-learning-3653430. [Image]. Pixabay.* https://pixabay.com/photos/never-stop-learning-3653430/

Altmann, G. (2019). *Presentation-woman-training-4608263. [Image]. Pixabay.* https://pixabay.com/illustrations/presentation-woman-training-4608263/

Amy. (2018). *Vintage-retro-steampunk-steam-punk-3160785. [Image]. Pixabay.* https://pixabay.com/illustrations/vintage-retro-steampunk-steam-punk-3160785/

Furtado, A. (2018). Woman-surrounded-by-sunflowers-raising-hand-1261459/. [Image]. Pixabay. https://www.pexels.com/photo/woman-surrounded-by-sunflowers-raising-hand-1261459/

Hain, J. (2014). Brain-mind-mindset-reality-544412. [Image]. Pixabay. https://pixabay.com/illustrations/brain-mind-mindset-reality-544412/

Hain, J. (2015). Self-self-image-image-identity-792365. [Image]. Pixabay. https://pixabay.com/illustrations/self-self-image-image-identity-792365/

Pete, D. and. (2018). Paper-document-business-composition-3111146. [Image]. Pixabay. https://pixabay.com/photos/paper-document-business-composition-3111146/

Productions, R. (2020). Healthy-fashion-people-woman-6539938. [Image]. Pixabay. https://www.pexels.com/photo/healthy-fashion-people-woman-6539938/

Riccardo. (2016). Woman-sitting-on-gray-rock-near-body-of-water-185801. [Image]. Pixabay. https://www.pexels.com/photo/woman-sitting-on-gray-rock-near-body-of-water-185801/

Siric, J. (2017). Woman-wearing-black-long-sleeved-shirt-sitting-on-green-grass-field-691919. [Image]. Pexels. https://www.pexels.com/photo/woman-wearing-black-long-sleeved-shirt-sitting-on-green-grass-field-691919/

Storm, S. (2014). 123-let-s-go-imaginary-text-704767. [Image]. Pexels. https://www.pexels.com/photo/123-let-s-go-imaginary-text-704767/

Venita, O. (2016). Flower-butterfly-banner-web-1283602. [Image]. Pixabay. https://pixabay.com/illustrations/flower-butterfly-banner-web-1283602/

Vogel, G. (2018). Wellness-carafe-purple-towel-3715860. [Image]. Pixabay. https://pixabay.com/photos/wellness-carafe-purple-towel-3715860/

Woman-using-gray-laptop-computer-in-kitchen-1251833. (2017). [Image]. Pixabay. https://www.pexels.com/photo/a-woman-in-purple-long-sleeves-smiling-while-wearing-eyeglasses-8307324/

Yoga-woman-lake-outdoors-2176668. (2017). [Image]. Pixabay. https://pixabay.com/photos/yoga-woman-lake-outdoors-2176668/

Made in the USA
Las Vegas, NV
14 March 2024

87190305R00132